Madison Cawein

Red Leaves and Roses

Poems

Madison Cawein

Red Leaves and Roses
Poems

ISBN/EAN: 9783744685153

Printed in Europe, USA, Canada, Australia, Japan

Cover: Foto ©Thomas Meinert / pixelio.de

More available books at **www.hansebooks.com**

Red Leaves and Roses

Poems

BY

MADISON CAWEIN

AUTHOR OF "LYRICS AND IDYLS," "DAYS AND DREAMS,"
"MOODS AND MEMORIES," ETC.

G. P. PUTNAM'S SONS
NEW YORK LONDON
27 West Twenty-third St. 24 Bedford Street, Strand
The Knickerbocker Press
1893

COPYRIGHT, 1893
BY
MADISON CAWEIN

Printed and Bound by
The Knickerbocker Press, New York
G. P. PUTNAM'S SONS

TO
MY MOTHER

PROEM.

OH, shall I sing of joy I only
    Remember as departed joy?
Of life once glad that now is lonely?
    Of love a treasure, now a toy?
Of grief, regret but makes the keener,
    Of longing disappointment mars?—
These will I sing, and sit serener
    Than song among the stars.

Or shall I sing of faith once spoken?
    Of vows heart-happy once with tears?
Of promised faith and vows long broken
    One hath remembered many years?
Of truth, the false but leaves the truer,
    Of trust, the doubt makes doubly sure?—
These will I sing, the noble doer
    Whose dauntless heart is pure.

I will not sing of time made hateful,
    Of hope that only clings to hate;
Of charity now grown ungrateful,
    And pride that cannot stand and wait.—
Of humbleness care hath imparted,
    Of resignation born of ills,
These will I sing, and stand high-hearted
    As hope upon the hills.

Once on a throne of gold and scarlet
    I touched a chord and felt it break;
I dreamed I was a king—a varlet
    A king's amusement left to wake.—
Now on a star my longing lingers,
    While on a tomb I lean and read,
And write with eager soul and fingers
    That life may give me heed.

CONTENTS.

	PAGE
Red Leaves and Roses	1
Wild-Thorn and Lily	7
The Idyl of the Standing-Stone	38
Some Summer Days	47
An Epic of South-Fork	55
A Niello	66
Wreckage	70
Hieroglyphs	78
Siren Sands	87
At the Lane's End	93
Deep in the Forest	101
One Night	115
The Elixir of Love	119
The Spell	123
The Return	125
The Letter	127
Wounded	129
The Parting	131
The Daughter of the Snow	133
Hildegard	136
Urganda	139
The Son of Evrawc	143
Torquemada	157
An Episode	163
The Mameluke	166
The Slave	168

	PAGE
The Seven Devils of Mahomet	170
John Davis, Boucanier	172
Thamus	176
Adventurers	179
Voyagers	180
America	182
The Ocklawaha	184
The Minorcan	187
The Spring in Florida	189
Strategy	191
The Whippoorwill	193
Satan	195
Sic Vos Non Vobis	196
Once	198
Resignation	200
After Rain	202
Peace	205

RED LEAVES AND ROSES.

I.

AND he had lived such loveless years
   That suffering had made him wise;
And she had known no truer tears
   Than those of girlhood's eyes.

And he, perhaps, had loved before—
   One who had wed? one who had died?
So life for him had been but poor
   In love for which he sighed.

In years and love she was so young
   Youth paused and beckoned at the gate,
And bade her list love's birds that sung;
   She said that love should wait.

One understood. One only knew
   The fields were faded, skies were gray,
Nor saw the sad rose autumn blew
   There in her heedless way.

II.

If he had come to her when May
Danced down the wildwood,—every way
Marked with white flowers, as if her gown
    Had torn and fallen,—it might be
She had not met him with a frown,
    Nor used such love so bitterly.

Or if he had but come when June
Set stars and roses to one tune,
And breathed in honeysuckle throats
    Clove-honey of her spicy mouth,
His soul had found some sunny notes
    In hers to cheer the cloudy South.

He came when Fall made mad the sky,
And on the hills leapt like a cry
Of battle; when the leaves were dead;
    To find a dreamy blonde in white,
Thrust in whose hair one rose, blood-red,
    Glowed like the Summer's heart of light.

He might have known, since leaves were blown,
And in the woods great weeds were grown;
Since nearing Winter wrecked the world,
    How love like his would seem absurd
To her whose sinless lip had curled,
    Yet heard him to his latest word.

Still he was humble, and denied
His tongue that instant's flush of pride,
For he remembered how the gray
   Held heaven and earth, alas! and knew
She wore the colors of the May,
   And to the May her heart was true.

And so he left her: and the bud
In her deep hair—one drop of blood
Out of his life to weaken him :—
   Again (the poison of his pain),
Poppy, for her to crush and brim
   A goblet with, that he must drain.

III.

"Such days as these," one said, and bent
   Among the marigolds, all dew,
And dripping zinnia stems, "are sent
   Out of the days our childhood knew;
And it is these endearing those,
   So dearer now they are grown old;
Days, once imperfect with the rose,
   Sufficient with the marigold."

"Such days as these," one said, and gazed
   Long with unlifted eyes that held
Sad autumn nights, "our hopes have raised
   In futures that are mist-enspelled.

And so it is the fog blows in
    Days dearer through the death they paint
One hard surrendering of sin
    One long ability to saint."

IV.

Gold deeds of hearts that have not kept
    Rare riches as a miser, when
Pale lips have writhed and eyes have wept
    Among the toiling tribes of men,
Each summer day gave man sweet alms
    Of silver in white lilies, while
Each night, with healing, outstretched palms
    Stood Christlike with its starry smile.

Will she remember this when dull
    Months drag their sadder hours by,
With feet that crush the beautiful
    And leave the beautiful to die?
Or never see? nor sit with lost
    Dreams withered 'mid the empty husks,
And wait, neglectful of the frost,
    In dead delusions of the dusks?

V.

He is as one who, treading salty scurf
    Of lonely sea-sands, hears the roaring rocks

Of some lost isle of misty crags and lochs;
Who sees no sea, but, through a world of surf,
   Gray ghosts of gulls and screaming petrel flocks:

When from the deep's white ruin and wild wreck,
   Above the fog, beneath the ghostly gull,
   The iron ribs of some storm-shattered hull
Looms, packed with pirate treasure to the deck
A century rotten: feels his wealth replete,
   When long-baulked ocean claims it; and one dull
Wave flings derisive at despondent feet
   A skull, one doubloon rattling in the skull.

VI.

And when full Autumn sets the dahlia stems
   On fire with flowers, and the chill dew turns
   The maple trees, above geranium urns,
To Emir tents, and strings with flawless gems
   The moon-flower and the wahoo-bush that burns;
Calmly she sees the year grow sad and strange,
   And stands with one among the wilted walks
Of the gray garden of the stern stone grange,
   And feels no sorrow for the frost-maimed stalks
   Since—though the wailing Autumn by her walks—
Youth marks swift Spring on life's far mountain-range.

Or she will lean to her old harpsichord;
   A youthful face beside her; and the glow

Of hickory on the hearth will baulk the blow
Of blustering rain that beats the casement hard ;
　　And sing of Summer and so thwart the snow.

" Haply, some day, she yet may sit alone,"
　　He thinks, " within the shadow-saddened house,
When on the gables stormy echoes moan,
　　And in the closet gnaws the lonesome mouse ;
And Memory come stealing down the stair
From dusty attics where is piled the Past—
Like so much rubbish that we hate to keep—
And turn the knob ; and, framed in frosty hair,
A grave forgotten face look in at last,
And she will know, and bow her head and weep."

WILD-THORN AND LILY.

I.

THAT night, returning to the farm, we rode
  Before a storm. Uprolling from the west,
Incessant with distending fire, loomed
The multitudes of tempest ; towering, here
A shadowy Shasta, there a cloudy Hood,
Veined agonies of gold aurora-born
Sierras of the storm. Vibrating on,
Low rumblings of the thunder far away ;
The opening welkin shone one livid sheet,
And all the firmament hung hewn with fire ;
Then leapt the thunder ; and it seemed that hosts
Of Heaven rushed to war with blazing shields
And swords of splendor. Through the driven trees
The large drops fell around us as we rode
Along the locust avenue. And she—
Was it the lightning that made weariness
Of her dim countenance? or memory
With the regret, that, now the thing was done,
A yearning fell upon her to be free,
Because she loved him better than she knew,
And must look backward on a barrier
That intervening months had built between
The possible and impossible? God knows ! . . .

Yet, I had won her honestly with words
Love only uttered out of its soul's truth,
Her, when engaged to Julien. What else
Had led us to elopement? Well; 't was done,
The whole, mad, lovely, miserable affair.
Who would avoid the consequence? Not I!
"Since she is only woman, I am man,
Strong with the fixed determination to
Bear all the blame and burthen willingly."

.

Scarce had we entered when high Heaven oped
Vast gates of gold and doors of booming brass
That dammed a deluge, and the deluge poured.—
I thought of him then; for I felt that she
Was thinking hard of Julien and his moods;
My school friend Julien, whom she once had won
To so believe she loved, and— Well! my play
Was open as the morning, and as fair.
His poverty and genius here, and here
My wealth and platitude; and I had won.
But it was hard for him. I did not dream
That it would end so. And when Gwendolyn
Used every tenderness—and that is much—
I did not dream his easy temperament
Were so effected of a wrong or right;
His character, intensely sensitive,
Would fall into extremes of morbidness,
And egoism. Far different my own,
Whose vigorous iron should not bend, but break

At one decisive blow: his should have sprung
Elastic as fine-tempered steel that bends
And so resumes its usual usefulness . . .
A wan smile strained the corners of her mouth
When from the porch into the parlor's blaze
I led her. And her mother met us there,
Her mother and her father. And I saw
The slow reflection of their happiness
Gain in her eyes, as their approval grew
From half-severe rebukes that were well meant.
She had done well, and we were soon forgiven.

But I resumed his letter when alone;
His letter written her three months before.
She had not read, and never should behold.
I would not let the dead scrawl mar and soil
My late-won joy, my testament of love.
No! I should read it, and I would destroy.
Thoughts made of music for a last farewell,
When he knew all and asked her to perpend
Expressions of past things her gift of love
Had given speech to in the happy days.
And so I read:—

II.

"The rhyme is mine, but yours
The thought and all the music, springing from
The rareness of the love that dawned on me
A little while to make my sad life glad.

Should I regret the sunset it refused,
Since all my morn was richer than the world?
Or that my day should stride without a change
Of crimson, or of purple, or of gold,
Into the barren blackness where the moon
And all God's stars lay dead? Should I complain,
Upbraid or censure or one moment curse,
I with my morning? 'T is a memory
That stains the midnight now: one wild-rose ray
Laid like a finger pointing me the path
I follow, and I go rejoicingly.

Our love was very young (nor had it aged—
If we had lived long lifetimes—once in me),
When one day, strolling in the sun, you spoke
Words I perceived should hint a coming change:
I made three stanzas of the thought, you see;
But now 't is like the sea-shell that suggests,
And will associate us with the sea
In its vague song and elfland workmanship.
Yet it has lost a something that it had
There by the far sand's foaming; something rare,
A different beauty like an element:

> I wonder on what life will do
> When love is loser of all love;
> When life still longs to love anew
> And has not love enough:—
> I'll turn my heart into a ray,
>   And wait a day.

I wonder on what love will hold
When life is weary of all life ;
And life and love have both grown old
With scars of sin and strife :—
I 'll change my soul into a flower,
    And wait an hour.

I wonder on why men forget
The life that love made laugh ; and why
Weak women will remember yet
The life that love made sigh :—
I 'll sing my thought into a song,
    And wait——how long?

III.

" And once you questioned of our mocking-bird,
And of the German nightingale, and I,
Knowing a sweeter bird than those sweet two,
Made fast associates of birds and brooks
And learned their numbers. Middle April made
The path of lilac leading to your porch
A rift of fallen Paradise ; a blue
So full of fragrance that the birds that built
Among the lilacs thought that God was there,
And of God's goodness they would sing and sing,
Till each new note led to diviner song.
And waiting by the gate, that reached the lane,
For you who gave sweet eloquence to all,
The sunset and the lilacs and the spring,
My heart was singing and it sang of you :

Two glowworms are the jewels in
Her ears, and underneath her chin
A diamond like a firefly :
There is no starlight in the sky
When Gwendolyn stands in the maze
Of woodbine of the portico,
For all the stars are in her gaze,
   The night and stars I know.

A clinging dream of haze the lawn
She wears ; and like a bit of dawn
Her fan with one red jewel pinned :
Among the boughs there breathes no wind
When Gwendolyn comes down the path
Of lilac from the portico,
For all the breeze her coming hath,
   The beam and breeze I know.

Two locust-blooms her hands, and slips
Of eglantine her cheeks and lips,
Her hair a hyacinth of gloom :
The balmy buds give no perfume
When Gwendolyn draws near to me,
The gate beyond the portico,
For all sweet essences is she,
   The fragrance that I know.

Life, love, and faith are in her face,
And in her presence sleep's soft grace ;
Her speech is my religion,—word
Of God I hear ;—no mocking-bird,

When Gwendolyn is by, may float
One bubble from the portico,
For all the birds nest in her throat,
　The song-birds that I know.

IV.

" The mocking-bird! And then weird fancy filled
My soul with vision, and I saw a song
Pursue a bird that was no bird—a voice
Concealed in dim expressions of the Spring,—
Who sits among the forests and the hills,
With dark-blue eyes that muse upon the flowers,—
Where we strolled anxious as the April hills:

The sunbeam, all the day that fell
　Upon the fountain,
Like laughter gurgling in the dell
　Below the mountain,
Drank, with its sparkle, one by one
The water words that seemed to run
A melody,—the sunrays tell,—
　That never yet was done.

The moonray, on the rocks that lay
　Where silence dallies,
Where Echo haunts the wilder way
　Among the valleys,
The livelong night upon the rocks
Hung, hid among girl Echo's locks,

To steal her voice,—the moonbeams say,—
  That mocks and only mocks.

The shadow, lain where shadows meet
  Beneath the roses
And thorns—the bitter and the sweet
  That life discloses,—
Hugged with the rose-balm and the dew
The crimson thorns that pierced it through;
The mad unrest,—the shades repeat,—
  That now is false, now true.

A fairy found the beam of gold,
  And ray of glitter;
The shadow whose dark bosom's fold
  Held sweet and bitter;
And made a bird beneath the thorn,
Dark gray to haunt the night and morn,
A voice of laughter,—it is told,—
  Love, mockery, and scorn.

v.

"Among the white haw-blossoms, where the creek
Droned under drifts of dogwood and of haw,
The red-bird, like a crimson blossom blown
Against the snow-white bosom of the Spring,
The chaste confusion of her lawny breast,
Sang on, prophetic of serener days,
As confident as June's completer hours.

And I stood listening like a hind, who hears
A wood-nymph breathing in a forest flute
Among gray beeches of myth-haunted ways:
And when it ceased, the memory of the air
Blew like a syrinx in my brain: I made
A lyric of the notes that men might know:

>Fly out with flirt and fluting—
>   As flies a falling star
>From flaming star-beds shooting,—
>   From where the roses are.
>
>Wing past, and sing me seven
>   Songs of faint fragrances
>White sylphs have breathed in heaven,
>   Or what such sweetness is.
>
>Sing on ! each burning feather
>   Thrill, throbbing at thy throat ;
>A song of glowworm weather,
>   And of a firefly boat :
>
>Of red morns and a princess
>   Who, changed to a perfume,
>Hid where yon lily winces,
>   Or where yon roses bloom.
>
>No bird calls half so airy,
>   No bird of dusk or dawn,
>O masking King of Fairy,
>   O red-crowned Oberon !

VI.

" Alas! the nightingale I never heard.
Yet I, remembering how your voice would thrill
Me with exalted expectation, felt
The placid-throated nightingale would win
Into my soul in some soft way like this:
Presentiments of nights that match the flowers
With the prompt stars and wed them with a song.
Of such, love whispered me when deep in dreams,
I made my nightingale.   It is a voice
Heard in the April of our year of love :

> Between the stars and roses
> There lies a summer-haunted lea,
> Where every breeze that blows is
> Another melody;
> Where every bud that pineth,
> Except the rose, divineth
> Each star is but a bee,
> Or golden moth that shineth.

> The star and rose are wiser
> Than all but love beneath the skies,
> For they are what the skies are
> And love hath made them wise :
> No bee may hum and rifle,
> No moon-moth come and stifle,
> The love that never dies,
> The love that will not trifle.

There is a bird that carries
Song messages; and comes and goes
'Tween every star that tarries
And every rose that blows:
A bird that will not tire,
Whose throat 's a throbbing lyre
To sing each star a rose,
And every rose a fire.

VII.

" O Maytime woods! O Maytime lanes and hours!
How should she know? But often of a night
Beside the path where woodbine odors blew
Between the drowsy eyelids of the dusk,—
When, like a swarm of pearly moths, the moon
Hung silvering long windows of her room,—
I stood among the shrubs. The dark house slept.
I looked and listened, for—I know not what . . .
Some tremor of her gown: a velvet leaf's
Unfolding to caresses of the spring;
A rustle of her footstep; like the dew
That rolls avowal from a tulip's lips
That burn with scarlet; or the whispered word
Of something lovelier than new leaf or dew—
The word young lips half murmur in a dream:

Serene with sleep light visions load her eyes,
   And underneath her window blooms a quince.
The night is a sultana who doth rise

In slippered caution to admit a prince,
Who her black eunuchs and her lord defies.

I dream that dreams besiege her, while the breeze
    Pelts me with petals of the quince and lifts
The Balm-of-Gilead buds, and seems to squeeze
    Aroma on aroma through sweet rifts
Of Eden, dripping through the rainy trees.

Along the path the buckeye trees begin
    To heap their hills of blossoms. Oh, that they
Grew Romeo ladders where her windows win
    The moonlight and the odor—that must pray
About her soul—so I might enter in!

A dream, to see the balsam scent erase
    Its dim intrusion; and the starry night
Conclude majestic pomp; the virgin grace
    Of every bud abashed before the white,
Pure passion-flower of her innocent face!

VIII.

" And once, in early May, a brush-bird sang
Among the garden bushes; and you asked
If the suave song stayed knocking at my heart.
I smiled some answer, and, behold, that night
Found that my heart had locked this fancy in:

    Rain, rain and a ribbon of song
        Uncurled where the blossoms are sprinkled;

The brush-sparrow sings, and I long
For the silver-sweet throat, that has tinkled,
To sing in the bloom and the rain,
Sing again, and again, and again,
   Under my window pane.

Rain, rain and the trickling tips
Of the million pink blooms of the quinces;
And I hear the song rill from her lips,
The lute-haunted lips of my princess:
O girl in the rain and the bloom,
Sing again in the pelting perfume,
   Sweetheart, under my room!

Rain, rain and the dripping of drops
From the cups of the blossoms they load, or
Leave laughing, on tipsiest tops;
And eyes of the sunbeam and odor:
There, under the bloom-blowing tree,
A face like a flower to see,
   Love is looking at me.

IX.

"Once in the village I had heard a song,
A melody that I would bring and sing
If such amused you. But, among your hills,
Majestic sunsets and the serious stars
Made discord of its words, that seemed as stale
As musty parlors where the village moped.

Look, lovely eyes, and let me know
 The timid flower, her love hath cherished,
Fades not before the fruit shall show,
Seen in the pure truth of your glow
 Whence all distrust hath perished.

Lift, winsome lips, and let me take
 The sacred whisper of her spirit
To mine in kisses, that shall make
Mute marriage of our souls, and wake
 High faith that shall inherit.

X.

" And so I wrote another filled with birds,
Deliberate twilight and eve's punctual star ;
And made the music of that song obey
The metre of my own and melody :

Only to hear that you love me,
 Only to feel it is true ;
Stars and the gloaming above me,
 I in the gloaming with you.
Staining through violet fire
 A twilight of poppy and gold,
Red as a heart with desire,
 Rich with a secret untold.

Deep where the shadow is doubled,
 Deep where the blossoms are long,

Listen!—deep love in the bubbled
   Breath of a mocking-bird's song.
Dearest, to know you are dearer,
   Drawing the skies from afar! . . .
Stars and the heavens the nearer
   By but one maiden—my star.

XI.

" Confronted with the certainty that I
Had no approval but my prompting hope's,
Who had not dreaded disappointment there!
The shadow of a heart's unformed denial,
That should take form and soon confirm the
    doubt!
The doubt that would content itself with this:

   If I might hold her by the hand,—
   Her hands so like the hands of Peace,—
   Her heart would hear and understand
      My heart's demand,
   And all her idling cease.

   If she would let my eyes look in
   Her eyes with all the look of Truth,
   Her soul might see how mine would win
      Her, without sin,
   In all her lovely youth.

   If I might kiss her mouth, and lead
   The kiss up to her eyes and hair,

There is no prayer that so could plead,—
    And find sure heed,—
My love's divine despair.

XII.

" And uninstructed smiled and wrote ' despair.'
Severe, yet eager of the shade that should
Some day come stealing through my silent door
To sit unbidden through the lonely hours.—
But now 't was summer, and all living things,
The lowly flowers and the common bees,
Became divine interpreters for me :

Say that he cannot tell her how he loves her,—
    Words of much adoration often fail,—
When but a lock that loosens, glove that gloves her,
    Clothe her coy femininity in mail.

So many humble wisdoms to express what
    The language of devotion is denied ;
Ambassadors to make the woman guess what
    Her heart's surrendered fortress hath defied.

A bird to bruit his bashfulness—perpend him !
    A bee to lisp the secret that is she ;
His pure appeal the blossom to defend him . . .
    Resistless pleaders, bird and bloom and bee.

XIII.

"So was my love acknowledged. For I thought
You loved me as love led me to believe:
And then, no matter where I walked or went
Among the hills, the woods, or quiet fields,
All had a poetry so intimate,
So happy and so ready that for me
'T was but to stoop and gather as I went;
As one goes reaching roses in the June.
Three withered wild ones that I gathered then
I send you now. Their scent and bloom are dust:

1.

What wild flower shows perfection
    As perfect as thy features are,
I leave to the election
    Of each deciding star:
Wild morning-glory or (who knows?)
Wild phlox, wild snowdrop or wild rose?

What cascade hath suspicion
    Of sparkle such as eyes like these,
I leave to the decision
    Of each proclaiming breeze:
The wind that kisses buds awake,
And rolls the ripple on the lake.

What bird shall sing the naming
    Of all the music that thou art,

I leave to the proclaiming
   Of my electing heart :
My heart, whose love is as thy soul
An infinite, adoring whole.

2.

What witch then hast thou met,
Who wrought this amulet ?
The charm that makes each look, love,
   A bud that blows ;
Thy face an open book, love,
   Whose language is the rose,
Than wisdom wiser yet.

What fairy of the wood,
To whom thou once wast good,
Gave thee this gift ?— Thy words, love,
   Should be pure gold ;
Thy voice as singing birds, love,
   Out of the Mays of old,
Whom love hath still pursued.

What goblin of the glade
This white enchantment made,
That haunts thy maiden presence
   As might the moon ;
Thy throat's, thy hand's white essence
   Of starlight soft with June
Upon a cool cascade ?

What wizard of the cave
Hath made my soul thy slave?
To dream of thee when sleeping,
   And when awake
My anxious spirit keeping
   'Neath spells that will not break,
Until thy love shall save!

3.

Dear, (though given conclusion to),
Songs, no memory surrenders,
Still their music breathe in you;
Silence meditation renders
Audible with notes it knew.

Heart, when all the flowers are dead,
Perfumes, that the soul remembers
Were included in their red,—
Making June of long December,—
From your hand and face are shed.

Dear, when night denies a star,
Darkness will not suffer, seeing
Song and fragrance are not far;
Starlight of the summer being
In the loveliness you are.

XIV.

"Revealing distant vistas where, I thought,
I saw your love stand as 'mid lily blooms,
Long angel goblets molded out of stars,
Pouring aroma at your feet: and life
Took fire with thoughts your soul must help you
    read:

A song; and songs (who doth not know?)
    Reveal no music but is thine.
Thou singest, and the waters flow,
    The breezes blow, the sunbeams shine,
    And all the sad earth is divine.

Low laughter; and I look away;
    The day may drowse, the night may dream,
I walk beneath sweet skies of May
    On ways where play the bud and beam,
    And hear a bird and forest stream.

A thought—and then it seems to me
    Lost lifetimes 'mid the stars arise,
Rain memories of the Heaven on thee;
    And it may be from Paradise
    Hast felt an angel lover's eyes.

XV.

"But is it well to tell you what I thought
When I beheld no change beyond the moods

That gloomed and glistened in your raven eyes?
When I sat singing 'neath one steadfast star
Of morning with no phantoms of strange fears
To slay the look or word that helped me sing:
When song came easier than come buds in spring,
That make the barren boughs one pomp of pearls;

    Oh, let the graceless day go past,
    And let the night be full of song.
    When life and life are one at last,
        And love no more shall long,
    'T is sweet midsummer of the dream,
        And all the dreams thou hast
    Are nearer than they seem.

    Once thou didst dream in autumn of
    Death with cadaverous eyes that gazed
    Deep in a shadow. . . It was love
        Whose beaming eyes were raised
    From the crowned sorrow that unrolled
        Strange splendor; and amazed,
    Love didst thou then behold.

    And we should know now, it is said,
    The dead are nearer than we know.
    And when they tell thee I am dead
        Thine eyes shall see it so;
    But I shall feel in every beat,
        And soul-song of thy woe
    My love live more complete.

XVI.

" One evening I would have you talk with me.
Impatience hurt me in your short replies.
And I who had refused,—because we dread
Approaching horror of our lives made maimed,—
The inevitable, could not help but see
Some secret change was here.—That night I
    dreamed
I wandered 'mid old ruins, where the snake
And scorpion crawled in poison-spotted heat;
Plague-bloated bulks of hideous vine and root
Wrapped fallen fanes; and bristling cacti bloomed
Blood-red and death-white on forgotten tombs.
And from my soul went forth a bitter cry
To pierce the silence that was packed with death
And pale presentiment. And so I went,
A white flame beckoning before my face,
And in mine ears sounds of primordial seas
That boasted preadamic gods and men:
A flame before and far beyond a voice:
But, lo, the white flame when I reached for it
Became thin ashes like a dead man's dust;
And when I thought I should behold the sea,
Stagnation, turned to filth and rottenness,
Rolled out a swamp; the voice became a stench.

    If we should pray together now
        For sunshine and for rain,
    And thou shouldst get fair weather now,

And I the clouds again,
Would rain and ray keep single,
Or for the rainbow mingle?

Dear, if this should be made to me,
  That I had asked for light,
And God had given shade to me,
  And thou shouldst know no night,
Would all thy daylight tarry?
Or night and morning marry?

If God should give me winter, love,
  And give thy life the spring,
And icicles should splinter, love,
  While all the wild birds sing,
Would thine walk by and glitter,
Forgetful mine is bitter?

XVII.

"So on the anguish of a dying hope
A baby hope was nourished; all in vain.
For at the last, although we parted friends,
The friendship lay like sickness on my soul,
That saw all gladness perish from the world,
And love build up a sepulchre for hope.

  And could you learn forgetfulness,
    And teach my heart how to forget;
  And I unlearn all fretfulness,

And teach your soul that still will fret ;
The mornings of the world would burn
Before us and we should not turn,
    For we should not regret.

Could you but know why sorrow treads
    Upon the heels of joy alway ;
And I how each to-morrow treads
    With shadowy steps upon to-day ;
No change or time would then surprise
Our lives with what our lives were wise,
    But one should see and say.

If you could stand exterior with
    Your dreams that still exalt desire ;
And I could live superior with
    The soul that makes my thoughts aspire ;
Long stairways would the stars unroll
To lift our love up, soul by soul,
    To some celestial fire.

XVIII.

" There fell no words of comfort from your lips.
Not that I asked for pity ; that had been
As fire to the scalded or dry bread
Unto the famished fallen 'mid the sands !
But all your actions said that I was wrong,
And how, I know not and have ceased to care ;
Still standing like one stricken blind at noon,

Who gropes and fumbles feeling all grow strange
That once was so familiar; cursing God
Who locks him in with darkness and despair.—
Your judgment had been juster had it had
A lesser love than mine to judge.—O love,
Where lay the justice of thy judge in this?—

  'If thou hadst praised thy God as long
As thou hast praised my hands and eyes,
Think of the sweetness of the song
  That now has only sighs!
Think of the trust that had been strong!
  The hope that had been wise!

  'If thou hadst bade my heart be more
Than life, because thy life was sad,
Thou hadst had all till I were poor
  To make thy sorrow glad.
Thou cam'st a beggar to my door,
  And had more than I had.

  'If thou hadst showed me how to love,
Nor played with love as children play,
The dove had still remained the dove,
  And never flown away.
My love is, and shall be, above
  The love that lasts a day!'

XIX.

" And haply it was this: One soul, that still
Demanded more than it could well return;
And, searching inward, yet could never pierce
Beyond its superficiality.
You did not know; but I had felt in me
The rich fulfilment of a rare accord,
And could not, though the longing lay like song
And music on me, win your soul's response:

    Were it well, lifting me
      Eyes that give heed,
    Down in your soul to see
    Thought, the affinity
      Of act and deed?
    Knowing what naught may tell
      Of heart and soul?
    Yet, were the knowledge whole,
      And were it well?

    Were it well, giving true
      Love all enough,
    Still to discover new
    Depths of true love for you,
      Infinite love?
    Feeling what naught may tell
      Of heart and soul?
    Yet, were the knowledge whole,
      And were it well?

XX.

" What else but, laboring for some good, to lift
Ourselves above the despotism of self,
All egoism strangling strength and hope!
Art, our intensest and our truest love,
Immaculateness that has never sped
Beyond her lover with his love all soul.
I followed beauty, and my ardor prayed
Your features would be blotted from my brain,
Nor mar the gratitude I owed to God.
I prayed; and see!—the influence of your eyes!—

    I have no song to tell thee
        The love that I would sing;
    The song that should enspell thee,
    The words that should so quell thee
        That all thy life would cling
    Around my heart to-morrow—
    For all my songs are sorrow.

    My strength is not a giant
        To hold thee with strong hands,
    To make thee less defiant,
    Thy spirit more compliant
        With all my love demands:
    Alas! my love is meekness,
    And all my strength is weakness.

    What hope have I to hover
        When wings refuse to rise—

To wing to thee, my lover,
Where all the nights discover
  No darkness like thine eyes ;
When life and hope lie dreaming
On thee who art but seeming !

XXI.

" I prayed ; and for a time felt strong as strength,
And held both hands out to the loveliness
That lured in the ideal. And I felt
Compelling power upon me that would lift
My face to heaven to behold the sun,
And bend it back to earth to see the flowers.
I learned long lessons 'twixt a look and look :

Breezes and linden blooms,
  Sunshine and showers ;
Rain, that the May perfumes,
  Cupped in the flowers :
Clouds and the leaves that patter
  Beryls of greenest glare ;
Wet rifts of skies that scatter
Sapphires the Sylphides shake,
When their loose fillets break,
  Out of their radiant hair.

Oh, for some song and lute !
  Wings that should pinion
Song for Love's swift pursuit

In Youth's dominion !
  Searching in all serenest
    Hours and buds and eyes,
  Saying, ' O thou who queenest
  Hearts, from thy lovely land
  Reach me no hidden hand
    Over the worldly wise ! '

XXII.

" Thus would I scatter grain around my life
To lure cloud-colored doves into my soul,
And find them turn black ravens while they flew.
The old, dull, helpless aching at the heart,
As if some scar had turned a wound again.
While idle grief stared at the brutal past,
Which held a loss that made the past more rich
Than Earth's rich arts : that marvelled how it came
Such puny folly should usurp love's high
Proud pedestal of life that held your form
In sculptured Parian lying strewn in shards.
And oft I shook myself,—for nightmares weighed
Each sense,—and seemed to wake ; yet evermore
Beheld a death's-head grinning at my lips.

So when the opening of the door doth thrill
  My soul with sudden knowledge he is come,
I shall remember and forget them still,
  The rough ways of the coarser world, until
His lips bend to me and my lips are dumb.

Then I shall not remember : but shall leave
    All recollection to the worldly race
My fact hath so accomplished.   Let them grieve
    The pale bereavements that do not bereave,
And in new epochs take my higher place. . . .

Who knocks?—The night scouts every hill and
    heath ;
    And round my door are minions of the night ;
And like a falchion, riven from its sheath,
    The wind swings, and the tempest grinds black
        teeth
Around me and my wild, hand-hollowed light.

Who knocks ? the door is open !—And I see
    The midnight groping with distorted fists
To throttle courage hurled upon her knee ;
    Hold high my candle, for it so may be
Love is bewildered in the rainy mists.—

No wandering wisp, to haunt the gusty rain
    With brimstone flicker, fading as it flies !—
The door is open ; will he knock again ?
    The door is open ; shall it be in vain ?
And ceremony still delay the wise ?

Who knocks in darkness waits till tempests pass.
    The door is closed : but morning lights shall thrust

It open : and the sun shall shine and mass
   White splendor where once stained a colored glass,
And toil and time—motes in a little dust."

   .   .   .   .   .   .

XXIII.

And I had read, read to the bitter close ;
Half hearing lone surmises of the rain
And trouble of the wind. At last I rose
And went to Gwendolyn. She did not know
The kiss I gave her had a shudder in it ;
Nor how the form of Julien rose between
Me and her lips, a bullet in his heart.

THE IDYL OF THE STANDING-STONE.

I.

SHE knows its windings and its crooks.
    The wild flowers of its lovely woods,
    The trumpet-vine's Red-Riding-Hoods,
The lily's story books;
    The iris, whose blue bonnets let
    Mab faces laugh from many a net
Along the fairy brooks.

He knows its shallows and its pools,
    The rugged stairs of rock that go
    Climbing through water-fall and flow,
Where haunt the minnow schools;
    The grass and sedge where haunts the snipe,
    The bob-white where the berry's ripe,
And whom the echo fools.

She seeks the bleeding-heart and phlox,
    The touch-me-not whose bushes fill
    The old stones of the ruined mill;
She wades among the rocks;
    Her feet are rose-pearl in the stream;
    Her eyes are blossom-blue; a beam
Gleams on her light-brown locks.

He comes with fishing bait and line
   To angle in the darker deeps,
   Where all the sounding forest sleeps
Of sycamore and pine;
   And now and then a shadow swoops
   Around him of a hawk or groups
Of pearl-gray clouds that shine.

And will he see, if they should meet,
   How she is fairer than each flower
   Her apron fills? and in that hour
Feel life is incomplete?
   He stops below; she walks above—
   The brook one blossom, white as love,
Floats fragrant to his feet.

And she—should she behold the tan
   Of manly face and honest eyes,
   Would her heart know nobilities
To make him more than man?
   She drops one blossom—has she heard
   Soft whistling of a man—or bird,
Whose dreamy quavers ran?

They knew; but then—they did not meet;
   Yet some divulging influence
   Had touched them with the starry lens
God holds to make hearts beat;

That made her heart one haunting wish,
And his—forgetful of the fish,
One flower at his feet. . . .

II.

The sassafras twigs had just lit up
   The yellow stars of their fragrant candles,
And the dog-wood brimmed each brown-stained cup
   With April the brown bough dandles ;
When down the orchard, whose apple blooms—
   Say, Ho, the hum o' the humble bee !—
Were woven of morn on the elfland looms,
A sense of Spring in the sprinkled glooms,
   A glimpse of the Spring—'t was she.

The maple as red as the delicate flush
   Of an afterglow where the west was crimson ;
And the red-haw tree in the wing-whipped hush
   With its milk-white blossoms and greening limbs on ;
And up in the wood where the oak-tree strung,—
   Say, Heigh, the rap o' the sapsucker !—
Gray buds in bunches, as if they hung
The fairies' belfries with bells that swung,—
   Was he with a heart for her.

Ay ! white the bloom of the rattle-weed,
   And white the bloom of the plum and cherry :
And red as a stain the red-bud's brede,

And a flower the color of sherry;
And he saw her in the orchard drift,—
  And, ho! the dew from the web that slips!—
And she saw him in the woodland rift;
And he had given his life to lift
  Her pure face to his lips.

And the plantain there as odorous as
  The heliotrope in his mother's garden;—
When the beam from the hollow did seem to pass,
  And the ray on the hills to harden;
For she had smiled, and the sun fell flat,—
  And, heigh, the wasp i' the pawpaw bell!—
And she had beckoned—and more in that
To him than Spring on her hills who sat,
  Or the wide white world could tell.

III.

The teasel and the horsemint spread
  The hillsides with pink sunset thrown
  On earth around The Standing-Stone
That ripples in its rocky bed:
  There are no treasuries that hold
  Gold richer than the daisies' gold
That crowd its mouth and head.

Deep harvest, and a mower stands
  Among the morning wheat and whets

His scythe, and for a space forgets
The labor of the ripened lands;
   Then bends, and through the dewy grain
   His cradle hisses, and again
He swings it in his hands.

And she beholds him where he mows
   On acres whence the water sends
   Faint music of reflecting bends
And falls that interblend with flows;
   She stands among the old bee-gums,
   Where all the apiary hums,
A simple bramble-rose.

She hears him whistling as he leans
   To circling sweeps the rabbits fly,
   And sighs and smiles and knows not why,
Nor what her heart's sweet secret means:
   He rests upon his scythe and sees
   Her smiling 'mid the hives of bees
Beneath the flowering-beans.

The peacock-purple lizard creeps
   Along the fence-rail; and the drone
   Of insects makes the country lone
With dreaming where the water sleeps:
   She hears him singing as he swings
   His scythe; he thinks of other things
Than toil and, singing, reaps.

IV.

Song.

Into the woods they went again
   Over the fields of oats ;
A reaper he and the binders twain,
Out of the acres of golden grain
   In where the lily throats
Were brimmed with the summer rain.

Hung on a bough a reaper's hook,
   Over the fields of oats ;
And a maiden here with a merry look,
And a laugh that rippled out of the brook,
   Out of the wild birds' throats,
For the kiss that the reaper took.

Out of the woods the reaper went
   Over the fields of wheat,
And a binder by with a face that blent
All of life that is innocent,
   All of love that is sweet,
Writ in her soul's young testament.

Who the maiden to keep the tryst,
   Over the fields of wheat?
She, his folly had only kissed?
She, he had given, to kiss whose wrist,
   His whole strong life made sweet?
She who had seen and wist?

V.

Her only pearls are beads of hail,
Her only diamonds are the dews ;
Such jewels never can grow stale,
   Nor any value lose.

Among the millet beards she stands ;
The languid wind lolls everywhere ;
There are wild roses in her hands,
   One wild rose in her hair.

To-morrow where the shade is warm
Among the June-ripe wheat she'll stop,
And from one daisy-loaded arm
   One yellow daisy drop.

She meets his brown eyes, glad and grave,
With blue eyes where the dreams are sweet ;
He is her lover and her slave,
   And mows among the wheat.

When buds broke on the apple trees
She wore an apple-blossom dress,
And walked with him on clover leas,
   And made him guess and guess.

When goose-plums ripened in the rain
Plum-colored was her gown of red ;

They strolled along the creek-road lane—
  He had her heart she said.

When apples thumped the droughty land
A russet color was her gown.
A hunter came, and wooed her hand,
  A stranger from the town.

When grapes hung purple in the hot,
They missed her dark-blue hood and dress;
And one tanned vintager forgot
  The purple of the press.

When snow made grave-stones of each sheaf
Her gown was whiter than the snow,
Her rubies redder than the leaf
  The autumn forests know.

What wounds her splendid shame conceals—
Men will but kiss her if she sigh
And never ask. And she?—she feels
  How all her life 's a lie. . . .

VI.

In spring the hairy-vetchling strewed
Blue morning blots on moss and leaf,—
The little Esau of the wood
Whose soul sat smiling in its grief:—

In spring he looked along the earth—
No month, he thought, holds so much grace,
No month of spring, such grace and mirth,
As the true April of her face.

In fall the frail gerardia
Hung signs of sunset and of dawn
On root and rock, as if to draw
Eyes ere the careless feet pass on.—
And will you blame her in pursuit
Of butterflies, who does not dream
A flower loosened by her foot
Drifts helpless with her down the stream?

SOME SUMMER DAYS.

I.

IF you should find her standing there
  Among the tiger-lily blooms,
That lose rich jewels everywhere
Among the woodland gleams and glooms,
You would confess her over-fair,
A cousin of the wood's perfumes.

The afternoon is dead with heat ;
And all the drowsy shadow sleeps
Like toil arm-pillowed in the wheat
Beside the scythe with which he reaps :
A blazing knight whose arms defeat
The shades, the day rides down the deeps.

There is no sound more distant than
The bell that haunts the hazy hill ;
No nearer than the locust's span
Of sound that makes the silence shrill ;
And now there comes a sun-brown man
Through tiger-lilies of the rill.

And they will go ; and in the end
The west will glow, the east will pale,
And then the glow and pallor blend

Like moonlight on a shifting sail ;
And in the woods he 'll speak and bend
His tan-dark face that laughs a tale.

The dusk will flash and fade away
Through heavy orange, rose, and red,
And leave the heavens violet gray
Above a gipsy-lily bed ;
And they will go, and he will say
No words to her but love hath said.

Ten million stars the night will win
Above them, and one firefly
Pulse like a tangled starbeam in
The cedar dark against the sky ;
And he will lift her bashful chin
And speak, and she will not deny.

And when the moon, like the great book
Of judgment, golden with the light
Of God, lies open o'er yon nook
Of darkest hill and wildest height,
Together they will cross the brook
And reach the gate and kiss good-night.

II.

And oft he wipes his hand along
The beaded fire of his brow
Hard toil has heated ; and the strong

Face flushes fuller health as now
He fills his hay-fork with a song,
And, tossing it, again doth bow.

And now he stops to look away
Across the sun-fierce hills and meads
No rolling cloud has cooled to-day;
And from his face the brawny beads
Drip; and he marks the hills of hay,
The fields of maize, the fields of weeds.

He sees wild walls of tempest build
Black battlements along the west,
Black breastworks that are thunder-filled;
And bares his brow; and on his chest
The sweat of toil is cooled; and stilled
The pulse of toil within his breast.

A strong wind brings the odorous death
Of far hay-makings, and the scent
Is good within his nostrils' breath;
The mighty trees are bowed, that leant
For none yet, as when Power saith
"Bow down!" and stalwart slaves are bent.

He laughs, long-gazing as he goes
Along the elder-sweetened lane:
He feels the storm wind as it blows

Across the sheaves of golden grain,
And stops to pull one bramble-rose,
And watch the silver slanting rain.

And there among low trees the farm
Dreams in a martin-haunted place ;
He marks the far-off streaks of storm
That with the driven thunders race ;
He sees his baby on her arm,
And in the door her smiling face.

III.

Below the sunset's range of rose,
Below the heaven's bending blue,
Down woodways where the balsam grows,
And milk-weed tufts are gray with dew,
A Jersey heifer stops and lows ;
The cows come home by one, by two.

There is no star yet ; but the smell
Of hay and pennyroyal mix
With herb-aromas of the dell
Where the root-hidden cricket ticks ;
Among the iron-weeds a bell
Clangs near the rail-fenced clover-ricks.

She waits upon the slope beside
The windlassed well the plum-trees shade,
The well-curb that the goose-plums hide ;

Her light hand on the bucket laid,
Unbonneted she waits, glad-eyed,
Her dress as simple as her braid.

She sees fawn-colored backs among
The sumachs now ; a tossing horn
Some clashing bell of copper rung ;
Long shadows lean upon the corn,
And all the day dies insect-stung,
Where clouds float crimson skeins of yarn.

Below the pleasant moon, that tips
The tree-tops of the hillside, fly
The evening bats ; the twilight slips
Some fireflies like spangles by ;
She meets him, and their happy lips
Touch where glad glories drown the sky.

He takes her bucket, and they speak
Of married hopes while in the grass
The plum lies glowing as her cheek ;
The patient cows look back or pass,
While in the west one golden streak
Burns as if God gazed through a glass.

IV.

The skies are amber blue and green
Before the coming of the sun ;
And all the deep hills sleep serene

As pale enchantment, never done ;
The morning mists drag down or lean
On woods in which vague whispers run.

Birds wake; and on the vine-grown knob,
Above the brook, a twittering
Confuses songs day cannot rob
'The building birds of where they swing ;
And now a sudden throat will throb
Wild music, and the thrush will sing.

The sun is up ; the hills are heaped
With instant splendor ; and the vales
Surprised with shimmers that are steeped
In purple where the white mist trails ;
The water-fall, the rock it leaped,
Are burning gold that foams and fails.

He drives his horses to the plow
Along the vineyard slopes, that bask
Dew-beaded grapes, half-ripened now,
In sun-shot shafts the shadows mask ;—
He feels the morning like a vow
Of faith that helps him with his task.

Before him, soaring through the mist,
The wild hawk drifts gray wings and screams ;
Its dewy back gleams, sunbeam-kissed,
Above the wood that drips and dreams ;

He guides the plow with one strong fist ;
The soil rolls back in level seams.

Packed to the right the sassafras
Lifts leafy walls of spice that shade
The blackberries, whose tendrils mass
Big berries in the coolness made ;
They drop black ripeness on the grass
Where fallen trumpet-flowers fade.

White on the left the fence and trees
That mark the garden ; and the smoke
Uncurling in the early breeze ;
The roof beneath the acorn oak ;—
He turns his team, and turning sees
The damp, dark soil his coulter broke.

Bees buzz ; and o'er the berries poise
Lean-bodied wasps ; loud blackbirds turn
Across the corn ; there is a noise
Of eager wings and winds that burn ;—
And now he seems to hear her voice,
The song she sings to help her churn.

v.

There are no clouds that drift around
The moon's pearl-kindled crystal, (white
As some sky-summoned spirit wound
In raiment lit with limbs of light,)

That have not softened like the sound
Of harps when Heaven forgets to smite.

The vales are deeper than the dark,
And darker than the vales the woods
That mounting hill and meadow mark
With broad, blurred lines of solitudes :—
Far off a fox-hound bays and barks
Impatient of the calm that broods.

And though the night is never still,
Yet what we name its noises makes
Its silence :—now a whippoorwill ;
A frog whose hoarser tremor breaks ;
And now the insect sounds that fill
The hush ; an owl that hoots and wakes . . . .

They lean against the gate that leads
Into the lane that lies between
The yard and orchard ; flowers and weeds
Are odorous,—as if the keen
Scents day poured in hot leaves and seeds
Night's dews distil from out the green.

Their infant sleeps. They feel the peace
Of something done that God has blessed,
Soft as the pulse that will not cease
There in the cloud that haunts the west ;
The peace that love shall still increase
While soul in soul still finds its rest.

AN EPIC OF SOUTH-FORK.

I.

THE wild brook gleams on the sand and ripples
    Over the rocks of the riffle ; brimming
Under the elms like a nymph whose nipples
    Lift and vanish and shine in swimming ;
Under the linns and the ash-trees lodging,
    Loops of the limpid waters lie,
Shaken of schools of the minnows, dodging
    The sudden wings of the butterfly.

Lower, the loops are lips of laughter
    Over the stones and the crystal gravel ;
Lower, the lips are a look seen after
    Song and laughter that lips unravel :
Lengths of the shadowy water, shaken
    Of the dropping bark of the sycamore,
Where the water-snake, that the noises waken,
    Slides like a crooked root from shore.

Peace of the forest ; the peace made dimmer
    Than dreams. And now a wing that winnows
The willow leaves with their shadows slimmer
    In the shallow there than a school of minnows

Calm of the creek ; and a huge tree twisted,
    Ringed and turned to a tree of pearl ;
A gray-eyed man who is farmer-fisted,
    And a dark-eyed, sinewy country girl.

The brow of the man is gnarled and wrinkled
    With the weight of the words that have just been
        spoken ;
And the girl has smiled and her eyes have twinkled,
    Though the bonds and the bands of her love are
        broken :
She smiles, nor knows how the days have knotted
    Her to the heart of the man who says :
" Let us follow the paths that we think allotted ;
    I will go my ways and you your ways.

" And the man between us is your decision.
    Worse or better he is your lover.—
Shall I name him worse that the long Elysian
    Prize he wins where I discover
Only the hell of the luckless chooser ?—
    Shall I name him better or hold him more
Since he is winner and I am loser,
    His life 's made rich and mine made poor ?"

" I tell you now as I oft and ever
    Have told," she answered, the laughter dying
Down in her eyes, " that his words have never
    Held me so—but you think me lying,

And you are wrong. And I think it better
   To part forever than still to dwell
With the sad distrust, like an evil tetter,
   On our lives forever, and so farewell."

And she turned away ; and he watched her going,
   The girlish pride in her eyes a-smoulder :
He saw her go, and his limbs were glowing
   Fever that parched. And he stood, one shoulder
Slouched to the tree ; and he saw her stooping
   There by the bank with a cautious foot,
Straighten, and tear from her breast the drooping
   Lilies and fasten the Pleurisy-root.

With its orange fire he saw her passing
   On and on, and the blood beat, burning
His brain to blisters ; an endless massing
   Of wounds and bruises of deathless yearning.
—Butterflies sucked in the moist sand-alleys ;
   A fairy fleet of Ionian sails
Were their wings ; or the sails of pirate galleys,
   Maroon and yellow, for elfland gales.—

He watched her going ; and harder, thicker
   The pulse of his breath and his heart's hard throbbing.
—How should he know that her heart was sicker ?
   How should he know that her soul was sobbing ?

She never looked back : and he saw her vanish
  In swirls of the startled butterflies,
Like a storm of flowers, and could not banish
  The look of love from his face and eyes.

II.

He heard the cocks crow out the lonely hours.
  How long the night and very far the dawn !
It seemed long months since he had seen the flowers,
  The leaves, the sunlight, and the beehived lawn ;
Had heard the thrush flute in the tangled showers.

His burning eyes ached, staring at the black
  Stolidity of midnight.   Would it send
No cool reprieve unto his mind,—a rack
  Of inquisition,—tortures to unbend,
That stretched him forward and now strained him back ?

Invisible and sad and undivulged,—
  The thought that made him think of summer walks
Through woods on which the sudden perfumes bulged,
  The bird-songs and the brilliant-blossomed stalks ;
And that young freedom which their talk indulged.

Oh, strong appeal ! And he would almost yield ;
   When, firmly forward, he could feel her fault
Oppose the error of a rock-like shield,
   And to resisting phalanxes cry halt—
And, lo ! bright cohorts broken on the field.

O mulct of morning, to the despot night
   Count down unminted gold, and let the day
Walk free from dreadful dungeons, and delight
   Herself on mountains of the violet ray,
Clad in white maidenhood and maiden white !

A melancholy coast, plunged deep in dream
   And death and silence, stretched the drizzling dark,
Wherein he heard a round-eyed screech-owl scream
   In lamentation, and a watch-dog bark,
A voiced oblivion, at night's hollow stream.

And then hope moved him to divide the blinds
   To see if those bright sparkles were a star's
Or only his hot eyeballs', which the mind's
   Commotion weighed.—No slightest ravel mars
With glimmer heaven's swart tapestry he finds.

Yet he remained refreshed, until the first
   Exploring crevices of Aztec morn,

Dim cracks of treasure, Eldorados burst:
   Then could he face his cowardice and scorn
This weakness which his manhood had immersed.

It knew no barriers now. And where it went
   Each twisting path was musical with birds;
Each weed was richer with diviner scent;
   For love sought love with such expressive words
That dawn's delivery was less eloquent.

III.

Who is it hunts with his dog
   There where the heron is flying
Gray in the feathering fog
   Over the hillside that's lying,
There by the butternut log
   Where night heard the screech-owl crying?

Who is it hunts in the brush
   Under the linns and the beeches,
Here where the Fork is a blush
   In the rocks that the noon never reaches?
Here where the bank is a crush
   Of flags with a bloom like the peach's?

He is handsome and supple and tall,
   Blond-haired and vigorous-chested,
Blue-eyed as the bud by the fall

Where he listens,—his rifle half rested,
Half leaned on the crumbling stone-wall,—
   And his face, it rarely has jested.

He waits ; and the sun on the dew
   Of the cedars and leaves of the bushes
Strikes glittering frostiness through. . . .
   If a covey of partridges flushes
What good will a Winchester do,
   Or the dog to his feet that he crushes?

As something breaks strong through the weeds
   Where the buck-bushes toss and the higher
Snakeroot with its spiring seeds,
   Wild carrots, are trammelling wire
Round the path to the creek-road that leads . . .
   Shall he know, shall he see ere he fire ?

   . . . From the leaves of the wind-shaken wood
   Thick drops of the night-dew are falling.
He is gone from the place where he stood
   Just there where the black crow is calling.
There is blood on the weeds : is it blood
   Down the face of the man that is crawling ?

Red blood or a smudge of the dawn ?
   And he lies with his gray eyes wide staring
Stiff, still at the sun : he has drawn

His limbs in a heap: and the faring
Bee-martins light near and are gone :
　But the tomtit and wren, they are daring.

It is noon ; and the wood-dove is deep
　In the calm of its cooing ; and over
The tops of the forest trees sweep
　The shadows of buzzards that hover ;
The wild-hawk sails on as asleep,
　And the bob-white is whistling from cover.

It is dusk ; and the wild flowers wilt
　With the sadness of crime in their faces ;
The blue wild petunias tilt
　To the larkspur in death-darkened places ;
On the wild sweet-williams are spilt
　The sunset or guiltier traces ? '

It is night ; and the hoot-owlet mocks
　The dove of the day with weird weeping :
The creek is a groan 'mid the rocks
　Where the 'coon through the briers is creeping :
Through the woods snaps the bark of the fox—
　But the dead, they are deaf in their sleeping.

IV.

Night flies and day is here,—
　God's fairer ultimate
Of causes never clear

To lives that will not wait ;—
Day dies and night is near,
   And love is over-late.

A storm has rent great limbs,
   And bent the wooded ridge ;
Each swollen shallow swims
   Head-deep below the bridge ;
The drift, that breaks and brims,
   Floats lighter than the midge.

Dusk dies and night is gray
   With shadows and with rain ;
The forests sound and sway
   Like monsters wrenched with pain ;
Night deepens on the way—
   And shall she wait in vain?

The Fork is whirling wreck
   Of field and hill and wood ;
And many a moon-wan fleck
   Floats where the rock-fence stood ;—
A current rolls break-neck
   Above the washed-out blood.

Night deepens : and she waits
   Expectant in despair :
The Fork has reached the gates,

The wood's wreck everywhere.
Night deepens; and she hates
   The man that will not dare.

She sees the lightning rush
   Blaze-boiling hells above;
She hears the thunder crush
   Heaven as if devils clove—
Bowed in the lightning's flush
   Through wind and rain comes love.

He comes she feels, and stands
   The rushing waters o'er
Her feet, and on her hands
   And hair the rains that pour,
And sees the instant lands
   Light-looming from her door.

Night deepens; but she knows
   Love will not fail to send
Reprieve to her young woes,
   And one day's errors mend.—
The wild stream foams and flows
   In booming fall and bend.—

Again the lightnings light
   The night like some wild torch;
The waters foam and fight;

And one uprooted larch
Drives down, with something white
　Wedged in it, by her porch.

She stoops: the lurid rain
　Beats on her back and head—
Ay! he hath come again
　With livid lips once red!
A bullet in his brain
　The night hath brought him—dead!

A NIELLO.

I.

IT is not early spring and yet
   Of lamb's-tongue banks above the stream,
And blotted banks of violet
     My heart will dream.

Is it because the wind-flower apes
The beauty that was once her brow,
That the white thought of it still shapes
     The April now?

Because the wild-rose learned to blush
In tune with cheeks of maidenhood,
I find full Junetide in bare brush
     And empty wood?

Why will I think how young she died!—
Straight, barren death stalks down the trees,
The hard-eyed hours by his side
     That kill and freeze.

II.

When orchards are in bloom again
My heart will bound, my blood will beat,

To hear the red-bird so repeat
   On apple boughs his strain ;
His blithe, loud song, heard through the rain
In summer, now among the bloom,—
Where all the bees and hornets boom,—
   Inviting to remain.

When orchards are in bloom once more,
Evasions of dear dreams will draw
My feet, like some persistent law,
   Through blossoms to her door :
And I shall ask her, as before,
" To let me help her at the well " ;
And fill her pail ; and long to tell
   My secret, o'er and o'er.

I shall not speak until we quit
The farm-gate, buried in its stain
Of orchards all in bloom again,
   And see the wood-dove sit
And call ; and through the blossoms flit
The cat-bird crying while he flies ;
Then bashfully I 'll praise her eyes,
   And cheeks with gladness lit.

And it may be that she will place
Her trust in me as once before,—
When orchards are in bloom once more,—
   With all her sweet girl grace :

And we shall tarry till a trace
Of sunset dyes the heaven, and then—
To tell her all ; and bend again
   To kiss her quiet face !

And homeward, humming, I shall go
Along the cricket-chirring ways,
When all the west, one crimson blaze,
   Blooms as if orchards blow
Piled petals in it. I shall know
Glad youth once more and have her here,
Who has been dead this many a year,
   To make my old heart glow.

III.

I would not die when Springtime lifts
   The white world to her maiden mouth,
And heaps its cradle with gay gifts,
   Breeze-blown from out the singing south :
Too glad for death the wind and rain ;
   Too heedless for earth's wildest woe
The young hypocrisy of pain
   That will not let you know.

I would not die when Summer shakes
   Her daisied locks below her hips,
And, naked as a star that takes
   A cloud, into the water slips :

Too rich were earth for my poor needs
   In egotism of loveliness ;
The apathy that never heeds
   If grief be more or less.

But I would die when Autumn goes,
   The wild rain dripping from her hair,
Through forests where the wild wind blows
   Death and the red wreck everywhere :
Sweet as love's last farewells and tears
   To fall asleep in the sad days,
With patience and with faith that nears
   The mist that God shall raise.

WRECKAGE.

SUCH love has drifted out of dreams
    Under the moon of a Florida night,
Over the beach with its silver seams,
    White as a sail is white ;

Such days have entered into some lives
    Out of the love that the nights have borne,
Over the waves where the vapor drives,
    Mists that the stars have torn ;

Such songs have welded two hearts and hands
    Out of the sea and the summer moon,
Out of the stars and the mists and sands,
    Setting two lives in tune ;

Days of love and the love will keep
    Truth and hope and the faith as one—
Care will sing and the hate will weep
    Loss that the love begun.

    .   .   .   .

I.

Parting he said to her : " We are not true to them,
   Gifts of the seasons : the night and the morning,
Love and the loss of all love, that 's a clew to them,
   Trust that is hope, and a faith never scorning.
Have you considered the life that regretfully
   Foldeth weak arms to the fate it could master ?
Slave of all circumstance, sadly and fretfully
   Whines for the comfort that cometh no faster ? "

They had come down to the ocean that, bellowing,
   Boiled on the sand and the shells that were broken ;
All of the season was faded and yellowing ;
   All of their misery of love had been spoken.
It had befallen the heavens were lowering ;
   Over the sea, like the wraith of a wrecker,
Clamored the gull ; and the mist in the showering
   East seemed the ghost of a lofty three-decker.

Infinite foam ; and the boom of the hollowing
   Breakers that buried the rocks to their shoulders ;
Battle and boast of the deep in the wallowing
   World of the waves where the red sunset smoulders.
Long was the leap of the foam on the thunderous
   Beach ; and each end of the beach was a flying

Toss of the spray. "Let our cares vanish under
   us;
  Doing, be hope of us now, and not dying!"

Yet, if it came to the part he has said to her
  "Strive with and master?"—What grief could
     have striven,
Weaker than all that is woman, he dead to her,
  There in the weeds and the waves that are
     driven!
Where, in the morning, farewells they have taken,
     now
  Must be repeated with tears, though the sailor
Sailed with a laugh, that her kiss will not waken
     now,
  Sealed with the salt on the lips that are paler.

2.

All day the rain drove, falling
   Upon the sombre sea;
All day, his wet sail hauling,
   The sailor tacked a-lea;
And through the wild rain calling,
   I heard her calling me.

At dusk the gull clanged, drifting
   Above the boiling brine;
And, through the wan west sifting,

Streamed one wan sunset line;
And, to my gray eyes lifting,
   Her sad eyes gazed in mine.

All night the wind wailed, sighing
   Along the wreck-strewn coast;
All night the surf, defying,
   Rolled thunder in and boast;
All night I heard her crying,
   A ghost that called a ghost

3.

The balm of the night and the glory,
   The music and scent of the sea,
Are a part of our lives, and the story
   Of thee and of me.—
The stars of the night, and the whiteness
   Of foam on the stretch of the sand,
The foam that is flung, and the lightness
   Of hand within hand.

No sail on the ocean; no sailor
   On shore, and the winds all asleep;
And thy face in the starlight far paler
   Than women who weep.
A mist on the deep that was ghostly;
   A moon in the deep of the skies;
The mist and the moon, they were mostly
   In thee and thine eyes.

No sea-gull to vanish with gleaming
    Of wings, but the swing of the spray
And a sense of unutterable dreaming
       That bore me away.
No wind and no wing, but their essence,
    And all that is grayest and dim,
In the mermaiden grace of thy presence,
       In look and in limb.

That night of strange cries! and to perish
    So out of our lives that were bare,
Yet ached with the yearning to cherish
       With patience and prayer!
For thou wast a sea-mist made woman,
    And I was a sound of the sea
Made man—but nothing was human
       In thee and in me.

4.

And one had sought the deep that glasses
    The face of God and His majesty;
And one still sought the gulf that passes
       Life and its mystery.
Time and tears and the days that ever
    Burden the back of the days to be;
Strife and grief and the seas that sever
       Love in a ship at sea.

One had come where the reef rolled broken
   Foam of the baulked waves everywhere ;
Waves that tangle the weeds and oaken
      Wreck and a dead man's hair.
One had come where the sand laid livid
   Paths of ease which the sea-gulls share ;
The wing of the gull in the light less vivid
      Light than the gladness there.

Winds that gallop with strength and splendor
   Steeds of the surf with their streaming manes
Surf that batters the coast's defender,
      Surf that the rock disdains:
Storm that hunts in his sounding sandals,
   Hounds of thunder he holds with chains,
Light that leaps like the spear he handles,
      Storm and the rush of rains.

Wrenching the wreck of the world asunder,
   Black rebellion of hell and night ;
Wrath and roar of the rocks and thunder,—
      Might and the curse of might.—
Beating the drift and the hush together,
   Waves and wind that the morn makes white ;
Calm and peace of the dove-dyed weather,—
      Light and the grace of light.

Clouds blow by and the storm 's forgotten.
   Savage coasts where the sea-cow feeds.

Wash of weeds and the sea weeds rotten.
    And a dead face in the weeds.
None to know him or name him brother;
    Only the savage in feathers and beads;
The South Sea Islander, fitting another
    Flint in the shaft he speeds.

Clouds blow up and the sea-gulls gather;
    Clouds blow up and the evening falls;
The lightning leaps and the sad sands lather,
    Rolling the waves in walls:
Who shall tell her, sweetheart or sister,
    Her who sings as the tempest calls?
Suns that beat on his face and blister?
    Wind or the wave that crawls?

. . , ...

This was his hope: that, by the ocean sitting,
    Dawn would compel her grave eyes to behold,
Between the foam ridge and the sea-gull's flitting,
    His body rolled.

All was not as it was before they parted;
    She said she would remember, and forgot;
He said he would forget her, angry-hearted,
    And yet could not.

She never knew : and, had she known, she surely
   Had given pity when she could not give
Her love to him, who loved her madly, purely,
     And bade him live . . .

Between the seaweed and the rocks the slanted
   Hulk of a wreck : beyond the sand and wave,
Worn with the wind and with the cactus planted,
     His nameless grave.

HIEROGLYPHS.

1.

MY dreams are older than the trees,
  Being but newer forms of change ;
Some savage dreamed mine ; and 't was these
  De Leon sought where seas were strange.

My thoughts are older than the earth
  Being of beauty ages wrought ;
Old when creation gave them birth,
  When Homer sang them, Shakespeare thought.

2.

If souls could travel with their thought
Beyond the farthest arcs that span
Worlds of imaginative man,
  Where thought is lightning fraught ;
One would explore the stars, and one
The science of each moon and sun
    Long evolutions wrought.

And one would seek out Hell ; and, wise
In tortures of the damned, return
To tell us how they freeze or burn,
  And where God's red Hell lies;

And one would look on Heaven ; and, mute
With memories of harp and lute,
   Sit silent as the skies.

But I—on condor wings would sweep
Back to cosmogony, and sit
In firmaments volcano-lit,
  And see creation heap
The awful Andes, vague and vast,
Around the Inca-peopled past,
    While deep roared out to deep.

3.

Out of it all but this remains :—
I was with one who passed wide chains
Of the Cordilleras, whose peaks
Lock in the wilds of Yucatan,
Chiapas and Honduras. Weeks—
And then a city that no man
Had ever seen ; so dim and old,
No chronicle has ever told
The history of men who piled
Its temples and huge teocallis
Among mimosa-blooming valleys ;
Or how its altars were defiled
With human blood ; whose idols there
With stony eyes still stand and stare.

So old the moon can only know
How old, since ancient forests grow
On mighty wall and pyramid.
Huge ceïbas, whose trunks were scarred
With ages, and dense yuccas, hid
Fanes, and the cacti, scarlet-starred.
I looked upon its paven ways,
And saw it in its pride and praise,
When from the lordly palace one,
A victim, walked with prince and priest,
Who turned brown faces to the east
In worship of the rising sun :
At night ten thousand temple spires
On gold burnt everlasting fires.

Uxmal? Palenque? or Copan?
I know not. Only how no man
Had ever seen ; and still my soul
Believes it vaster than the three.
Volcanic rock walled in the whole,
Lost in the woods as in some sea.
I only read its hieroglyphs,
Perused its monster monoliths
Of death, gigantic heads ; and read
The pictured codex of its fate,
The perished Toltec ; while in hate
Mad monkeys cursed me, as if dead
Priests of its past had taken form
To guard their ruined shrines from harm.

4.

And then it was as if I talked
   Of flowers and beauty, like a God;
Mid Montezuma's priests who walked
   Obedient to my nod.

From Mexic levels breezes blew
   O'er green magueys, cacao fields;
I stood among caciques, a crew
   With plumes and golden shields.

In raiment made of humming-birds
   Brown slave-girls danced. All Anahuac
Stood, grim with strange obsidian swords,
   Around the idol's rock.

And up the temple's winding stair
   Of pyramid we wound and went.
The bloomed vanilla drenched the air
   With all its tropic scent.

Volcanoes walled us in; and I
   Walked crowned with flaming cactus-flowers,
Beneath the golden, Aztec sky,
   Lord of the living hours.

When, lo! five priests who led me to
   A jasper stone of sacrifice!—
Then deep within my soul I knew
   My pride's ignoble price.

A sixth priest, robed in cochineal,
    Received me at the altar's stone ;
I saw the flint-blade, sharp as steel,
    That in his high hand shone.

O God ! to dream that they would bind—
    With pomp and pageant of their love—
Me to the rock, and never blind
    Mine eyes to that above !

I felt the flint hack through my breast,
    And in my agony did raise
Wild eyes, a little while to rest
    Upon their idol's face.

Just God ! the priest tore out my heart
    To hold it beating to the sun—
And pain beheld Love's scarlet part
    In life that was undone.

Torn out, I felt my heart still beat—
    " How sweet to die if thou wert mine ! "—
My heart, cast at the idol's feet
    Knew that the face was thine !

5.

She was a maiden like a dream.
    She led me where volcanic dust

Rained in a scoriac mountain stream.
    The Andes rose in snow, or thrust
Black craters belching stones and steam.

She was an Inca princess when
    I was a cavalier of Spain,
Who frowned among Pizarro's men
    And watched the New World rent with pain—
No grace of God could save me then!—

And it was she who led me far
    To gaze on caves of Inca gold;
Until we came where, warrior
    On warrior, an army rolled
In savage panoply of war.

Fierce faces chiselled out of stone
    Were not so stern.—Down underneath
I heard the sullen earthquake groan;
    Above me, red eruptions seeth;
And set my teeth and stood alone.

And then she pled and was denied.—
    They laid me where the lava crawled
Red rivers down the mountain side.
    I felt the slow, slow hell-heat scald;
And as it closed, she leapt and died.

6.

In farther planets there are men who talk
With beaming eyes and brows that burn with thought;
Pure souls whose sentiments need but be born
To be expressed. Where speech of mouth and tongue
Were barbarous discord. Where no voice imparts
Thought, but divulging eye and sensitive brow.
Superior planets far beyond our sphere,
And nearer God than ages shall combine
To lift our world up with its wrangling woes.
Worlds that are strange to sickness and disease
Of mind or body; perfect mentally,—
Past what we name perfection here on Earth,—
And physically. Morally divine
As creeds have taught us God's high Heaven is.
Worlds where Love makes no playmate of vile Lust;
Where Hope makes no companion of Despair;
Where Power can not trample with fierce feet;
And, impotent, the iron hand of Might
Surrenders its red weapon unto Mind;
Where Truth and Thought are wedded, in one rule
Of far progressions, whose white child is Love.

So have I thought, and longed to leave sad Earth
To live anew on some sublimer sphere;
A world so higher, lovelier than is this,

So spiritually perfected and refined,
Should one behold, behold ! one would fall prone
In worship and astonishment ; and all
The exaltation of celestial peace
Declare within his soul, "Yea, this is Heaven !
How long, O sinner, hast thou dwelt in Hell !"

7.

An iron despotism the day's :
A brutal anarchy the night's :
What hope for hope when day betrays
    To night's ignoble spites !

For once I prayed for gulfs of gold,
And eve spread pools of sombre blood ;
Clean skies of stars, and skies behold—
    Malignant with the scud.

And so I marvel not that he,
Gray-haired and palsied, hugs his stove
While I my youth, which once was she,
    Have buried with my love.

8.

All thoughts of Nature are its forms :
Life, love and death : these God began :
Sun-systems that are still in storms,
Evolving worlds to perfect man.

Thoughts are the forms of Mind : and plumb
Effects to causes : Calculate
From intellect the mighty sum
Of truth as spirit ultimate.

SIREN SANDS.

I.

THE rhododendrons sleep and take
    The dew-drops they would weep away,
Among palmettoes of the lake
    Beyond the bay.

Shores where we watched the eve reveal
Her cloudy sanctuaries, while
The bay lay lavaed into steel
    For mile on mile.

We watched the purple coast confuse
Soft outlines with the graying light;
And towards the gulf a vessel lose
    Itself in night.

We saw the sea-gulls dip and soar;
The wild-fowl gather past the pier;
And from rich skies, as from God's door,
    Gold far and near.

Two foreign seamen passed and we
Heard mellow Spanish; like twin stars,
Where they lounged smoking we could see
    Their faint cigars.

Night; and the heavens stained and strewn
With stars dark waters realized,
Until their light the brightening moon
    Epitomized.

Night—but the pine-wood balms will wake;
Buds laugh the dew-drop from each face;
The bay will burn and on the lake
    The ripple race.

Far coasts detach deep purple from
The blue horizon, and the day
Behold the sunburnt sailor come
    To sail away.

The bird that dreamed at dusk, at dawn
Will sing again.—And who shall pine?
Not I! for thou, when night is gone,
    Wilt still be mine.

2.

Through halls of columned scarlet
  Like some dim queen, the Dusk
  Trails stately skirts of musk,
Hung in each ear a starlet,
  Weird jewels of the Jinn;
And golden 'neath her chin
  The moon, a gem-like tusk.

There lies a ghostly glory
　　Along the sea and sand,
　　That, like a knightly band
From lands of sacred story,
　　Kneels on the ray-red spray ;
A crusade stopped to pray
　　Beneath God's shielding hand.

Up flaming mountains millions
　　In burning pentecosts ;
　　Love's beauty-blinding hosts,
And radiance-raised pavilions
　　Among celestial flowers—
Earth's sense of angel hours,
　　The after ghosts of ghosts.

3.

Music that melts in moonlight,
　　Out of the summer breeze ;
Fireflies, moonlight, and foaming
　　Susurrus of the seas.

Music that drifts from perfume,
　　Soft as the touch of a hand ;
Dreams and stars and the ocean,
　　And two on the fluted sand.

Glimmers of vague reflections,
　　And the white flame of the foam

Pale on the purple a vessel,
    And a song to sing it home.

And I dream the dream of the music,
    And the firefly spark that floats,
For the music is glittering magic,
    And the flies are its golden notes.

And again you are singing the story
    Of the brown old coast and sea,
Of the lives that lived for passion,
    In an old-world melody :—

SONG.

"*Over the hills where the winds are waking*
    All is lone as the soul of me ;
Over the hills where the stars are shaking,
    Breton hills by the sea.

"*These were with me to tell me often*
    How she pined in her Croisic home,
Winds that sing and the stars that soften
    Over the miles of foam.

"*Fishers' nets and the sailor faces,*
    Sad salt-marshes and granite piers,
Brown, loud coast where the long foam races—
    And a parting full of tears.

" A gray sail's ghost where the autumn lies on
  Wraiths of the mist and the squall-blown rain ;
Her dark, girl eyes that search the horizon,
  Grave with a haunting pain.

" Stars may burn or the wild winds whistle
  Over the rocks where the sea-gulls rave—
My heart is bleak as the wind-worn thistle
  Dead on her sea-side grave." . . .

And I hear the harsh reef's hunger
  For a noble ship at sea,
And the voices of mermaids singing
  The sea's old tragedy ;

Till I am the doomed ship's pilot,
  And you are the mermaiden,
Who lures him on to the wrecking
  And into her arms again.

4.

Sad as sad eyes that ache with tears
The stars of night shine through the leaves ;
And barren as the nunlike years,
  The shades that darkness weaves.

The summer sunset marched long hosts
Of gold adown one golden peak,

That flamed and fell; and now gray ghosts
  Watch where the moon is weak.

Appealing years and eyes that weep;
Moon-mists that beckon or conceal;
Wan thoughts naught-medicines to sleep;
  Wan wounds that will not heal.

And heaven now hoarse with storm, that slips
Wild angles of the jagged light;—
I kiss the wild rain from her lips,
  And shield her from the night.

A moaning tremor in the trees;
And all the stars packed with black death;—
I hold her by the neck and knees
  And kiss away her breath.

Hell and hag Night drive on the rain;—
I hold her by the hair and plead:
She beats my face with blows again,
  With hands that burn and bleed.

The thunder plants deep cohorts on
The volleying heights—I should have known
How long it is that she is gone,
  And I how long alone!

AT THE LANE'S END.

1.

NO more to strip the roses from
    The rose-boughs of her porch's place!—
I dreamed last night that I was home
    Beside a rose—her face.

I must have smiled asleep—who knows?—
    The rose aroma filled the lane;
I saw her white hand's lifted rose
    That called me home again.

And yet when I awoke—so wan,
    An old face wet with icy tears!—
Somehow, it seems, sleep had misdrawn
    A love gone thirty years.

2.

The clouds roll up and the clouds roll down
Over the roofs of the little town;
Out in the hills, where the pike winds by
Fields of clover and bottoms of rye,
You will hear no sound but the barking cough
Of the striped chipmunk where the lane leads off;

You will hear no bird but the sapsucker
Far off in the forest,—that seems to purr,
As the warm wind fondles its tops, grown hot
Like the docile back of an ocelot;
You will see no thing but the shine and shade
Of briers that climb and of weeds that wade
The glittering creeks of the sun, that fills
The dusty road and the red-keel hills:
And all day long in the pennyroy'l
The grasshoppers at their anvils toil;
Thick click of their tireless hammers thrum,
And the wheezy belts of their bellows hum;
Tinkers who solder the silence and heat
To make the loneliness more complete.

Around old rails where the blackberries
Are reddening ripe, and the bumble bees
Are a drowsy rustle of Summer's skirts,
And the bobwhite's wing is the fan she flirts,
Under the hill, through the iron-weeds,
And blue mist-flowers and milk-weeds, leads
The path forgotten of all but one—
Where elder bushes are sick with sun
And wild raspberries branch big blue veins
On the face of the rock, where the old spring rains
Its sparkling splinters of molten spar
On the gravel bed where the tadpoles are,
You will find the pales of the fallen fence,
And the tangled orchard and vineyard, dense

With the weedy neglect of thirty years ;
The garden there,—where the soft sky clears
Like an old, sweet face that has dried its tears;—
The garden plot where the cabbage grew
And the pompous pumpkin ; and beans that blew
Balloons of white by the melon patch ;
Maize ; and tomatoes that seemed to catch
Oblong amber and agate balls
Thrown from the sun in the frosty Falls ;
The rows of currents and gooseberries,
And the balsam-gourd with its honey-bees ;
And here was a nook for the princess-plumes,
And the snap-dragons and the poppy blooms,
Mother's sweet-williams and pansy flowers,
And the morning-glory's bewildered bowers
Tipping their cornucopias up
For the humming-birds that came to sup ;
And over it all was the Sabbath peace
Of the land whose lap was the love of these ;
And the old log-house where my innocence died,
With my boyhood buried side by side.

Shall a man with a face as withered and gray
As the wasp-nest stowed in a loft away,
Where the hornets haunt and the mortar drops
From the loosened logs of the clapboard tops ;
That vice has aged, as the rotting rooms
The rain where memories haunt the glooms ;
A hitch in his joints like the rheum that gnars

In the rasping hinge of the door that jars ;
A harsh, cracked throat like the old stone flue
Where the swallows build the summer through ;
Shall a man, I say, with the spider sins
That the coarse years spin, in the outs and ins
Of his soul, returning to see once more
His boyhood's home, where his life was poor
With toil and tears and their fretfulness,
But rich with health and the hopes that bless
The unsoiled wealth of a vigorous youth ;
Shall he not take comfort and know the truth
In its threadbare raiment of falsehood ?—Yea !
In his crumbled past he shall kneel and pray,
Like a pilgrim come to the shrine again
Of the homely saints that shall soothe his pain,
And arise and depart made clean from stain !

3.

Years of care cannot erase
   Visions of the hills and trees
Closing in the dam and race ;
   Nor the mile-long memories
Of the mill-stream's lovely place.

How the sunsets used to stain
   Mirror of the water lying
Under eaves made dark with rain !
   Where the red-bird, nestward-flying,
Lit to try one bar again.

Dingles, hills, and woods and springs,
   Where we came in calm and storm,
Swinging in the grape-vine swings,
   Wading where the rocks were warm,
With our fishing nets and strings.

Here the road plunged down the hill,
   Under ash and chinquapin,—
Where the grasshoppers would drill
   Ears of silence with their din,—
To the willow-girdled mill.

There the path beyond the ford
   Takes the woodside, just below
Shallows that the lilies sword,
   Where the scarlet blossoms blow
Of the trumpet-vine and gourd.

Summer winds that sink with heat,
   On the pelted waters winnow
Moony petals, that repeat
   Crescents, where the startled minnow
Beats a glittering retreat.

Summer winds, that bear the scent
   Of the iron-weed and mint,
Weary with sweet freight and spent,
   On the deeper pools imprint
Stumbling steps the ripples dent.

Summer winds that split the husk
   Of the peach and nectarine,
Blow beyond the crimson dusk
   Hazy skirts, but faintly seen,
Spilling balms of dew and musk.

Where with balls of bursting juice
   Summer sees the red wild-plum
Strew the gravel ; ripened loose,
   Autumn hears the pawpaw drum
Plumpness on the rocks that bruise :

Here we found the water-beech,
   Some forgotten August noon,
With its hornet-nest in reach,
   Like a Fairyland balloon,
Full of bustling fairy speech.

Some invasion sure it was :
   For we heard the captains scold ;
Waspish cavalry a-buzz,—
   Troopers uniformed in gold
Sable-slashed,—to charge on us.

Could I find the sedgy angle,
   Where the dragon-flies would turn
Slender flittings into spangle
   On the sunlight? or would burn
Where the berries made a tangle,

Sparkling green and brazen blue?
   Rendezvoused about the stream
Turbaned gay banditti, who,
   Brigands of the bloom and beam,
Drunken were with honey-dew.

Could I find the pond that lay
   Where vermilion blossoms showered
Fragrance down the daisied way?
   And the sassafras embowered
Sap and spice of early May?

In the twilight might I seek
   The old mill! Its weather-beaten
Wheel and gable by the creek;
   And its warping roof; worm-eaten,
Dusty rafters worn and weak.

Where old shadows haunt old places,
   Loft and hopper, stair and bin;
Ghostly with the dust that laces
   Webs that usher phantoms in,
Wistful with remembered faces.

While the frogs' grave litanies
   Drowse in far-off antiphone,
Supplicating, till the eyes
   Of dead friendships,—long alone
In the dingy corners,—rise.

Moonrays or the splintered slip
   Of a star.—In twinkling darkle
Of the night the fire-flies dip—
   As if Night betrayed the sparkle
Of rich jewels through a rip.

And once more my boyhood crosses,
   With a corn-sack for the meal,
Through the sprinkled ferns and mosses,
   To the gray mill's lichened wheel,
Where the water drips and tosses.

DEEP IN THE FOREST.

I.

A COIGNE.

THE hills hang woods around, and green below
   Dark, breezy boughs of beeches mats the moss,
Crisp with the brittle hulls of last year's nuts;
The water hums one bar there; and a glow
Of gold lies steady where the trailers toss
Red, toppling bugles and a rock abuts;
In spots the wild-phlox and oxalis blow
Where beech roots bulge the loam, and welt across
The whole dense hillside in protruding ruts.

And where the sumach brakes grow dusk and
      dense,
Among the briers, yellow violets,
Lamb's-tongues and wind-flowers bloom; the
      agaric
In dampness crowds; a fungus, made intense
With gold and crimson and wax-white, that sets
The May-apples along the terraced creek
At gay defiance. Where the old rail-fence
Divides the hollow, there the bee-bird whets
His bill, and there the elder hedge is thick.

No one can miss it ; for two cat-birds nest,
Calling all morning, in the trumpet-vine ;
And there at noon the pewee sits and floats
A woodland welcome ; and his very best
At eve the blue-jay sings, as if to sign
The record of its loveliness with notes :
At night the moon stoops over it to rest,
And unreluctant stars ; where waters shine
There runs a whisper as of wind-swept oats.

II.

EVASION.

And shall I seek upon the hills
   For hints the orchards follow ?
Where wild-plum trees make wan the hills
   And apple-trees the hollow,
     Beneath the soaring swallow ?

In red-bud brakes and flowery
   Acclivities of berry ;
In dog-wood dingles showery
   With dew the sun makes merry,
     And drifts of swarming cherry ?

In valleys of wild strawberries,
   And of the white May-apple ;
Or cloud-like trees of hawberries,
   With which the south-winds grapple,
     And all the broad brook dapple ?

Whose eyes are dark forgetfulness,—
  To see the forest's daughter,—
Whose feet are bee-like fretfulness,
  Strive like a running water
  In boughs that kissed and caught her.

To see you, yet to find you not,
  To seek you and continue;
With hurrying hands that bind you not,
  Since one may never win you
  With striving soul and sinew.

In pearly, peach-blush distances
  Light limbs that have evaded
The eager heart's persistences,
  The rock-paved brook that waded,
  With chestnut branches shaded.

O presence, like the primrose's,
  Still hold me in your power!
With rainy scents of dim roses,
  That led me for an hour
  To find this one frail flower.

III.

THE WOOD-SPIRIT.

Ah me! I still remember
  How flushed, before the shower,
The dusk was, like a scarlet rose,
  Or blood-red poppy flower.

The heaven hath stars; the moonlight
  Lays blurs upon the grain—
You may not know it from white frost,
  The moonlight on the rain.

And all the forest utters
  A restless moan in rest,
For all the deep, dull shadow lies
  Like iron in its breast.

I mark the shocks of shadow,
  I mark the unmown corn,
The white, weird moonlight overhead—
  Would God I'd ne'er been born!

I sit alone and listen;
  The far leaves sound and sigh;
The dew drips from the bearded grain,
  The mist slips from the sky.—

I hear her whisper whispers,
  And breathe in yon gray place;
Her feet are easier than the dew,
  And than the mist her face.

She will not hear me, never!
  This spirit made for song,
Who dwelleth in the young, young oak,
  The old, old oaks among.

Her limbs are molded moonlight;
   Her breasts are silver moons;
She glimmers and she glitters where
   The purple shadow swoons.

And now she knows I love her,
   She says that I have died,
And laughs and dances in the mist
   That haunts the forestside.

When winds run mad in woodlands
   And mad the black rain sings,
I see her mad hair blow and blow
   Dark as a raven's wings.

When winds are tamed and tethered,
   And meadows bright as frost,
I will not walk within the wood
   For fear my soul be lost.

I seek her and she flees me;
   I follow through the mist—
The mist! the mist will freeze me dead
   Ere her shy lips be kissed!

IV.

OWL ROOST.

The slope is a mass of vines:
   If you walk in the daylight there,

A glimmering twilight shines
　'Neath vines that are everywhere;
Each trunk, that a creeper twines,
　Lifts strong and brown and fair
A column; and all is grave
As a cathedral nave.

No grass to carpet the feet:
　And the fox-grape tendrils lace
So thick that the noonday heat
　Is chill as a murdered face:
And the winds for miles repeat
　The fugue of a rolling bass:
The deep leaves twinkle and turn,
And jets of the sunlight burn.

A white-backed spider weaves
　Gray webs between the trees—
Witches who watch their sieves—;
　The honey and bumble-bees
Drop droning among the leaves—
　Fairies whose masks are these—;
At dusk the screech-owls croon—
Hobgoblins of the moon.

At dark I will not go
　Under its canopy
No glittering starbeams know;
　No new-moon hanging high,—

Like an Indian warrior's bow,
　With a star that seems to fly
The arrow of gold it shot :—
At dark I will not, will not!

At dawn, if my mood be dim,
　And the day be a cloudless one,
Under its leaf and limb
　I'll walk, though my heart doth shun
Its shade, and I feel the grim
　Horror of something done
Here in the years long past,
That God makes known at last.

v.

MOSS AND FERN.

Where bank the brakes of bramble there
　Wrapped with the trailing rose,
Through canes where waters ramble there,
　And where the wild pink grows—
　　　Who knows?
Beyond the reach of maid or man,
　　　Here's Pan.

Where, by the creek, whose pebbles make
　A foothold for the mint
The gray-blue flags like rebels make

A fallen rebel tint—
　　　A hint,
Since from the Old-World woods he ran,
　　　Of Pan.

Deep in the hollow of the hills
　　Ferns deeper than the knees ;
Long clouds drift down, that love the hills,
　　And bring the gradual breeze—
　　　　To please,
Since Syrinx fled beyond his scan,
　　　God Pan.

In woods whose beeches break upon
　　The peace like some wise word ;
Where sun-shot shadows shake upon
　　Our dream or flits a bird,
　　　　　You 've heard
The flute whose Grecian notes began
　　　With Pan.

Far in, where mosses lay for us
　　Still carpets of green plush ;
Where bloom and bee and ray for us
　　Burn on the budded flush,
　　　　　A hush
May sound the satyr hoof a span
　　　Of Pan.

In woods whose thrushes sing to us,
    And brooks dance sparkling heels ;
Whose wild aromas cling to us,
    While woodland worship kneels,—
        Who steals
Beside us, haunch and face of tan,
        But Pan !

VI.

WOODLAND WATERS.

Through leaves of the nodding trees,
Where creepers swing in the breeze
Red bag-pipes made for the bees,
    Whose slogan is droning and drawling ;
Where the columbine scatters its bells,
And the wild bleeding-heart its shells,
O'er mosses and rocks of the dells
    The brook of the forest is falling.

You can hear it under the hill
When the wind in the wood is still,
And, strokes of a fairy drill,
    Sounds the bill of the yellow-hammer:
By solomon's-seal it slips,
Cohosh and the grass that drips—

The laugh of an Undine's lips,
  The sound of its falls that stammer.

I doze in the woods: and the scent
Of the honeysuckle is blent
With the spice of a Sultan's tent,
  And my dream with the East's enmeshéd—
A slave girl sings; and I hear
The languor of lute-strings near,
And a dancing-girl of Cashmere
  In the harem of good Er Reshid.

From ripples of Irak lace
She flashes the amorous grace
Of her naked limbs and her face,
  While her golden anklets tinkle:
Then over mosaicked floors
Open seraglio doors
Of cedar: by twos, by fours,—
  Like stars that tremble and twinkle,—

While the dulcimers sing unseen,
The handmaids come of the queen,
'Neath silvern lamps, one sheen
  Of jewels of Afrite treasure:
And I see the Arabia rise
Of the Nights that were rich and wise,
Beautiful, dark, in the eyes
  Of Zubeideh, the Queen of Pleasure.

VII.

THE THORN-TREE.

The night is sad with silver and the day is glad with gold,
And the woodland silence listens to a legend never old,
Of the Lady of the Fountain, whom the fairy people know,
With her limbs of samite whiteness and her hair of golden glow,
Whom the boyish south-wind seeks for and the girlish-stepping rain,
Whom the sleepy leaves still whisper men shall never see again;
She whose Vivien charms were mistress of the magic Merlin knew,
That could change the dew to glow-worms and the glow-worms into dew.

There 's a thorn-tree in the forest, and the fairies know the tree,
With its branches gnarled and wrinkled as a face with sorcery;
But the Maytime brings it clusters of a rainy fragrant white,
Like the bloom-bright brows of beauty or a hand of lifted light.

And all day the silence whispers to the sunray of
   the morn
How the bloom is lovely Vivien and how Merlin is
   the thorn:
How she won the doting wizard with her naked
   loveliness
Till he told her demon secrets that but made his
   magic less:

How she charmed him and enchanted in the thorn-
   tree's thorns to lie
Forever with his passion that should never dim or
   die:
And with wicked laughter looking on this thing that
   she had done,
Like a visible aroma lingered sparkling in the sun,
Just to stoop and kiss the pathos of an elflock of
   his beard,
In the mockery of parting and mock pity of his
   weird:
How her magic had forgotten that "who bends to
   give a kiss
Will but bring the curse upon them of the person
   whose it is":
So the silence tells the secret.—And at night the
   fairies see
How the tossing bloom is Vivien, who is struggling
   to be free,
In the thorny arms of Merlin, who forever is the tree.

VIII.

THE HAMADRYAD.

She stood among the longest ferns
   The valley held ; and in her hand
One blossom like the light that burns
   Vermilion o'er a sunset land ;
   And round her hair a twisted band
Of pink-pierced mountain-laurel blooms ;
   And darker than dark dusks that stand
Below the star-communing glooms,
Her eyes and hair that shed perfumes.

I saw the silver sandals on
   Her pearl-white feet that seemed too chaste
To tread true gold : her face like dawn
   On splendid peaks that lord a waste
   Of solitude lost gods have graced ;
White arms and hands ; firm, faultless hips—
   Bound with the girdling silver, chased
With acorn cup and crown· and tips
Of oak-leaves—whence the chiton slips.

Limbs that the gods call loveliness !
   The grace and glory of all Greece
Wrought in one marble shape were less
   Than the perfection that were these.—

   I saw her; and time seemed to cease
For me—And, lo! I lived my old
   Greek life again of classic ease,
Barbarian as the myths that rolled
Me back into the Age of Gold.

ONE NIGHT.

I.

A NIGHT of rain. The wind is out.
   And I had wished it otherwise—
A wind to sweep the scudding skies
And burn big stars above the rout;
   Stars; and my eyes should meet her eyes;
   Confront the siren of her sighs;
The dimples of her cheeks that pout;
   Should see her calmness all surmise
   When I have said I love her lies—
And for that very love she dies.

II.

What breasts this wind has! As it runs
   Around each unprotected tree
   Its foggy eyes I seem to see,
Inhuman, yet a woman's ones;
   They blaze nor wink, as lionly
   As some bayed beast that will not flee
The pine knots and derides the guns.
   Or is it but the crime that 's she!
   Who makes such treachery of me,
   Dread substance of my phantasy?

III.

And now the boughs and whipping rain
    Confuse them . . . Ah ! her gaze is tense
    As song with lovely influence—
And it would pain to see her pain . . .
    Yet she must die—with every sense
    Strung to beholding knowledge, whence
My awful wound be whole again.
    The rain is dark ; the night is dense.
    Not with more silence Innocence
    Appeals to God than my defence.

IV.

And when she leaves (no one perceives !)
    The old gray manor where the eight
    Old locusts,—gnarly shadows,—freight
With mossy dreariness its eaves,
    One moment at the iron gate
    She 'll tarry. Then, with breath abate,
Come rustling through the autumn leaves.
    And I shall take both hands and sate
    My mouth on her's and say, " You 're late " ;
    She 'll laugh to hear I had to wait . . .

V.

O passion of lost vows, revive
    Imagination, and renew
    The ardor of love's language you

For love's rose-altar kept alive !
   Your priestly oaths that rang with dew
   And starlight !   Think that she is true
As beautiful.—But thought must thrive
   Here on her falseness, and pursue
   Deed with determined strength to do
The dastardy she drags me to . . .

VI.

And we shall walk before the wind ;
   The shuffling leaves about wet feet ;
   Our ruin as the wood's complete
Because one creature so has sinned
   And has not suffered.   She shall meet
   No murder in my eyes ; no heat
Of fate in holding hand that 's pinned
   To her's.   To make her trust to beat,
   I 'll kiss her hair, deep as deep wheat,—
Like affluent Summer's—saying " Sweet."

VII.

And should I bungle in this thing,
   This purpose that must leave her dead,
   And cure this fever in my head ?—
There is no wisdom that may bring
   Soul satisfaction, when is shed
   No redder blood than intent's red :
The baulked intention still will ring

Fiend noises ; voices that have led
Desire onward to be fed
With failure when success seemed said.

VIII.

When we have reached the precipice
   That mocks the battling of the sea,
   And wallows out black rocks, that knee
The giant surf and roar and hiss,
   I will not cease to coax and be
   The anxious lover. Trusting she
Will not suspect my farewell kiss
   Until it turns a curse, and we
   Sway for an instant totteringly,
   And she has shrieked some prayer at me.

IX.

O let me see no anguish there,
   No pain ! but terror and the frown
   Of crime's apprisal and renown
Of my life's injury, that bare
   This horror with its bloody crown !—
   No pity, Lord ! For if her gown,
Suspending looseness of her hair,
   Delay the plunge . . . the night is brown . . .
   My heel must crush her white face down,
   And Hell and Heaven see her drown.

THE ELIXIR OF LOVE.

" I HOLD it possible that he
   Who idolizes one that 's dead,
And dreams of her incessantly
   With visions toil has fed,
May cease and say, ' 'T is mine at last
To live and love the love that 's past ;
The joy without the grief and pain.
The dead shall live and love again.' "

And he had loved her till for him
   His love had grown an ideal part ;
He saw her standing fair and dim,
   Nor saw her withered heart :
And labored on ; for, truth to say,
His pleasure was not in the way
Of love accomplished, but love's thought
That justified the time he wrought.

And kept such trysts as phantoms keep,
   Pale distances about his soul ;—
And moved like one who walks asleep,
   Attaining no sure goal :
And blither than a lighter heart

At crucible and glass retort
He labored ; for his love was prism
To irisate toil's egoism.

He drained wan draughts from out a cup,
   A globe of vague and flaming gold,
Held from the darkness, brimming up,
   By something white and cold,
That touched faint lips against its brim,
Like flakes of foam ; and soft and slim,
Stooped out of fiery-bound abysses
To print his brow with icy kisses.

At last within his trembling hand
   An ancient flask burnt starry rose ;
The starlight of a lonely land,
   Whose mountains no one knows :
And in the liquid, like a flower,
A star-like face bloomed for an hour,
To slowly fade into a skull
That mocked all that was beautiful.

Though all his life had been so strange,
   Yet stranger than his life was she
Who led him from his room to range
   'Mid graves and mystery.
Who led him to her own sad tomb,
Where he could read within the gloom
The name of her who lay within
With all of silence, naught of sin.

Untainted, as it seemed, or made
   By skeleton kisses yet more fair ;
And thus he found her and so laid
   Her darkness depths of hair
Upon his shoulder ; and the pearls,
Around her neck and in her curls,
Not paler than the kingly calm
On brows and breasts without a qualm.

And through the night, beneath the moon,
   Across the windy hill, the gloom
Of forests where the leaves lay strewn,
   He brought her to his room :
And in the awfulness of death,
That filled her wide eyes with its breath,
He set her in a carven chair
Where the still moon could kiss her hair.

One moment stood as if to think ;
   Then to her lips, grown strangely red,
His fierce elixir pressed, and " Drink !
   Drink life and love ! " he said.
And if it drank—he did not know,
Absorbed upon the brow's wild woe ;
Or if it rose dispassionate,
With eyes of stone and lips of hate.

Still as Fall-frozen ice its face ;
And thin its voice as drizzled rain ;

And, coil on coil, on silk and lace
   Its quiet locks remain.
Nor breathed its bosom while it spake,
Like one whose mind is half awake,
Or lapsing to enchanted sleep
A century long in some old keep.

And stooping o'er it whispered low—
   A sound as soft as any lyre,
Or moonbeams beating on the snow
   An unavailing fire :—
"What is this life you give ?—Your toil ?
What is your love ? a thing to soil
Life with its unfulfilled desire ?—
There is no demon half so dire !"

And where before was quietness,
   Was violence and scorn and evil,
Yet all the form was passionless,
   A corpse that held a devil. . . .
And who shall say what hands were its
That made around his throat these pits,
That left him strangled ! or the one
Who placed by him this skeleton !

1886.

THE SPELL.

AND we have met but twice or thrice,—
    Three times enough to make me love!—
I praised your hair once and your glove,
Your foot, your gown—you were like ice;
    And yet this might suffice, my love,
    And yet this might suffice.

Saint John hath told me what to do:
If I can find the ferns that grow,
The fernseed that the fairies know,
To sprinkle fernseed in my shoe,
    And haunt the steps of you, my dear,
    And haunt the steps of you.

You 'd see the poppy-pods dip here,
The blow-puff of the thistle slip,
And no wind breathing—but my lip
Next to your anxious cheek and ear;
    And you would know me near, my love,
    And you would know me near.

On wood-paths I would tread your gown;
You 'd know it was no brier; then
I 'd whisper vows of love again,

And see your quick face flush and frown,—
    And then to kiss it down, my dear,
    And then to kiss it down.

You 'd muse at home, or read, or knit,
And know it was my hands that blotted
The page, or all your needles knotted,
And in your anger cry a bit;
    And I would laugh at it, my love,
    And I would laugh at it.

The secrets you should say in prayer,
Should I not know? or, should you sing,
The one you think of? or the thing
That makes you stare at empty air,
    And feel that I am there, my dear,
    And feel that I am there?

But when the whole sweet truth is said,
It is my soul that follows you;
It needs no fernseed in the shoe,—
Unless the heart's red love be dead,—
    To win you and to wed, my love,
    To win you and to wed.

THE RETURN.

A BROWN wing beat the apple leaves and shook
    One blossom on her hair. Then seemed to float
Deliberate bubbles. In her shaded book
She found romantic interest. No look
Betrayed the tumult in her trembling throat.

The bird sang on. A dreamy wind came down
From one white cloud of afternoon and fanned
The leaking petals on her book and gown
And touched her hair: she curved a quiet frown,
And smoothed it with a single-jewelled hand.

The ribbon of her hair dipped on her brow—
And then she knew he watched her: 'T was his
    breath
That moved the blossom on the apple bough;
His eyes that made the wood-thrush cease. And
    now
Her cheek went crimson, now as white as death.

Then on the dappled page his shadow; yes,
Not unexpected, yet her haste assumed

Fright's startle; and rich laughter did confess
His presence there, like some long-lost caress
Of noble manhood, where the thick trees bloomed.

Quickly she rose and all her gladness sent
Sweet welcome to him. Her his unhurt arm
Drew unresisted; and the soldier lent
Fond lips to hers. She wept. And so they went
Deep in the orchard toward the old brick farm.

THE LETTER.

LONG shadows towards the east ; and in the west
   A garnet conflagration, wherein rolled
One cloud like some great gnarly log of gold ;
Each gabled casement of the farm seemed dressed
In ghostly roses love made manifest.

And she had brought his letter here to read,
   Upon the porch, that faced the locust glade ;
   To watch the summer twilight burn and fade,
And breathe the dewy scent of wood and weed,
Forget all care and her sick soul to feed.

And on his face her fancy mused a while :
   Dark hair, dark eyes—" And now he has a beard
   Dark as his hair,"—she smiled ; yet almost feared,
It changed him so, she could not reconcile
Her heart to that which hid his lips and smile.

Then tried to feature, but could only see
   The beardless man who bent to her and kissed
   Her and their child and left them to enlist.
She heard his horse grind in the gravel. He
Waved them adieu and rode to fight with Lee.

And all around her drowsed the hushful hum
   Of evening insects. And his letter spoke
   Youthful caresses to her, nor awoke
One echo of the bugle or the drum,
But their whole future in one kiss did sum.

The stars were thick now; and the western blush
   Drained into darkness. With a dreamy sigh
   She rocked her chair.—It must have been the cry
Of infancy that made her rise and rush
To where their child slept, and to hug and hush.

Then she returned. But now her ease was gone.
   She knew not what, she felt some unknown fear
   Press tight'ning at her heart-strings; and a tear
Her eyelids scalded; and her cheeks grew wan
As helpless sorrow's, and her white lips drawn.

With stony eyes she grieved against the skies,
   A slow, dull, aching agony that knew
   Few tears, and saw no answer shining to
Her unasked questions from the stars' still eyes:—
"Where Peace delays and where her soldier lies?"

They could have answered. One was far away
   Beyond the field that belched black batteries
   All the red day: 'mong picket silences,
On woodland mosses, in a suit of gray,
Shot through the heart, one by his rifle lay.

WOUNDED.

IT was in August that they brought her news
  Of his bad wounds ; the leg that he must lose.
And August passed, and when October raised
Red rebel standards on the hills that blazed,
  They brought a haggard wreck that did abuse
  The youth whose strength their village had amazed.

An ailing spectre of the happy lad,
The five months husband, whom his country had
Enlisted, strong for war ; returning this,
Whose broken countenance she feared to kiss,
  While health's remembrance stood beside him sad,
  And wept for that which was no longer his.

They brought him on a litter ; and the day
Was glad and beautiful. It seemed that May
In woodland rambles had forgot her path
Of season, and, disrobing for a bath,
  By the autumnal waters of some bay,
  With her white nakedness had conquered Wrath.

Far otherwise she wished it : wind and rain ;
The sky, one gray commiserative pain ;

Sleet, and the stormy drift of frantic leaves;
Harsh frost and misery, that one perceives
   Has bit the hazel of her hair; again
   Has carved grave care around her mouth that
     grieves.

Theirs—a mute meeting of the eyes; she stooped
And kissed him once: one long dark side-lock
     drooped
Its braid against the bandage of his breast;
With feeble hands he stroked it and caressed,
   Then all his happiness in one look grouped
   Saying, "Now I am home, I crave but rest."

Once it was love! but then the battle killed
All that sweet nonsense of his youth, and filled
The heart with sterner madness.—Ah, well! Peace
Must blot it out with patience, whose surcease
   Is never hasty.—Yet, as God hath willed!
   With war or peace Who shapes wise ends at ease.

What else for them but, where their mortal lot
Of weak existence dragged rent ends, to knot
The frail unravel up!—Love (still afraid
Days will increase the burthen on it laid),
   Seeks consolation that consoleth not,
   And side by side with Sorrow waits the Shade.

THE PARTING.

SHE passed the thorn-trees, whose gaunt shadows tossed
Their sprawling spiders round her ; and the breeze,
Beneath the ashen moon, was full of frost,
And mouthed and mumbled in the sickly trees,
Like some starved hag who sees her children freeze.

Dry-eyed she waited by their sycamore.
Lone stars made misty blotches in the sky.
And all the wretched willows on the shore
Looked faded as a jaundiced cheek or eye.
She felt their pity and could only sigh.

His skiff had ground upon the river rocks.
Whistling he came into the shadow made
By that dead branch, from which the sea-gull mocks
The flood. And strong his boyish hands were laid
In hers. And she no weakness had betrayed.

Her speech was quiet while his greeting kiss
Stung through her hair. She did not dare to lift

The knowledge of her anguished eyes to his,
When tears smote crystal in her throat. One rift
Of heartache humored might set all adrift.

Anger and shame were his. She meekly heard.
And then the oar-locks sounded, and her brain
Remembered he had said no farewell word;
And hard emotion swept her, and again
Left her as silent as a carven pain. . . .

She, in the old sad farm-house, wearily
Resumed the drudgery of her common lot,
Regret remembering. . . .   'Midst old vices he,
Who would have trod on and somehow did not,
The wildflower, that had brushed his feet, forgot.

THE DAUGHTER OF THE SNOW.

THOUGH the panther's footprints show,
   And the wild-cat's, in the snow,
You will never find a trace
   Of the footsteps of a certain
Maiden with a paler face
   Than the drifts that fill and curtain
Hillside, valley, and the wood,
Where the hunter's wigwam stood
In the starving solitude.

What white beast hath grown the fur
For the whiter limbs of her?—
Raiment of the frost and ice
   To her supple beauty fitting;
Wampum strouds as white as rice,
   Mantle, of the frost's weird knitting,
Wrapping face and hair complete;
Fingers gloved with sparkle; feet
Moccasined with beaded sleet.

'Though he knew she made a haunt
Of the dell, it did not daunt:
Where the hoar-frost carved each tree
   Out of virgin alabaster,

And spun hairy bud and bee
   On each autumn-withered aster ;
By the frozen waterfall
He could hear the cold quail call
O'er the spangled chaparral.

Where the beech-tree and the larch
Built a shining triumph arch
For the morning marching down
   Hosts of silver-armored leaders ;
Where each hemlock had a crown,
   And huge diadems the cedars ;
Where the long icicle shone,
There he found her standing lone
Like a mist-wraith changed to stone.

And she led him many a mile
With her hand-wave and her smile,
And the printless swiftness of
   Feet of fog, and frosty flutter
Of her raiment ; now above
   Now below the boughs of utter
Winter whiteness. Led him on
Till the dawn and day were gone,
And the evening star hung wan. . . .

Hunters found him dead, they tell,
In the winter-wasted dell,

With his quiver and his bow,
   Where the cascade runs a rafter
Made of crystal and of snow ;
   Where he listened to her laughter,
Promises, that were as far
As the secrets of a star,
Leading on the warrior.

And her countenance is this
Haunting his ; and this the kiss
On faint mouth and fainter eyes
   Of her lip's divine December ;
This her triumph that defies
   Love the winter stars remember
Sought her, met her ; and 't is she
Clinging to him, neck and knee,
Where his limbs sank wearily.

HILDEGARD.

I.

IT was Hildegard who came
   From the forest of the mountain :
She whose hair is like the flame
   Of a sunset-fevered fountain :
You may know her by her eyes,
   Dauntless eyes of bitter beryl,
Where the anguish never dies,
   And the suffering soul sits sterile
In such haze as ever lies
   On the unsailed seas of peril.

II.

It was Hildegard. I knew
   By no sound or sight she trembled
Near me, lighter than the dew
   In the sessions of assembled
Flowers. Hers some influence
   Of soft, serpent magnetism,
Vanquishing my every sense
   With essential mesmerism ;
Holding me beneath the lens
   Of her will's compelling prism.

III.

I cannot escape.   She treads
    Noiseless as the forest flowers
Walked on by the wind ; their heads
    Pavements for the mottled hours :
She is brilliant as the trees
    Where young blossoms are unsheathing ;
She is lissome as the ease
    Of the woodland water's wreathing ;
She is subtle as the breeze
    Through the Summer's tresses breathing.

IV.

If she sings who is it hears
    But my spirit, that forever
Her strange singing moves to tears
    And to happy laughter never ?
Babylonian necromance,
    Oldest witcheries that arrow
Strains ensorcelling, and glance
    Through the life's bewildered marrow,
While the soul lies lost in trance,
    Helpless if such heal or harrow.

V.

She has bound me with her gaze,
    While her white hands weigh my shoulders ;
And my weak will swings and sways

To her gaze that burns and smolders.
She has led me far away
   Under boughs where Summer dallies:
Over peaks of purple day,
   Far away through Eden alleys:
Though the way be one long May
   It will end in Winter valleys.

VI.

Brazen earthquake treads the peaks;
   Iron skies are crusts that sunder,
Where the lightning's lava leaks
   Vomiting the hosts of thunder.
Still she kisses me.   Dark red
   With my heart's blood are her kisses:
Then her arms fall cold and dead,
   And my mouth her kisses misses—
She is gone; and in her stead
   Flies a milk-white snake that hisses.

URGANDA.

IT is Sir Elid of the Sword,
   Of whom King Lisuarte hath heard
These three long years no wished-for word.

His armor dofft, he comes in fur
And velvet, all the warrior,
And takes her hand and kisses her.

" Thrice have I heard the Summer sigh
For drowsy poppies that must die,
Seen sadder Autumn, fading, lie,"—

So said Helis and said with tears ;—
" Thrice welcome, Elid, though long years
Of silence fed my love with fears ! "

He said to her : " My own, my best,
To thee alone . . . *Witch! wilt thou wrest
This hour from me?* . . . shall be confessed
The thing that will not let me rest.

" It was at Hallowmas I spurred
Through woods wherein no wild thing
stirred,
No sound of brook, no song of bird.

" When softly down a tangled way
A dim fair woman, white as day,
Rode on a palfry misty gray.

" Upon her brow a circlet burned
Of jewels, and the fire inurned
Changed with her thoughts, and turned and
turned.—

" I stared like him, who, wild and pale,
Spurs, hag-led, through the night and hail.
When, lo ! adown a forest vale
An angel with the Holy Grail !

" It vanishes ; but, once beheld,
The longing heart is never quelled,
Its loveliness hath so enspelled.—

" She vanished. And I rode alone
Behind a voice that did intone,
' Urganda is she, the Unknown.

" ' And never shalt thou clasp the form
Of her who leads thee by a charm
To follow on through sun and storm.'

" I can not stay for weal or woe.
E'en now her magic bids me go,
Soft-summoning through wind and snow.". . .

Helis with sweetest songs beguiles
His hollow face until it smiles,
And with her lute shapes sweeter wiles :

Till kingly figures, woven in
The windy arras, seem to win
Strange, ghostly life, and slay and sin.

Until her deep hair's golden glow
Sweeps his dark curls as, praying low,
She kneels a marble-sculptured Woe.

'T were well to leave him here to rest,
Aweary with his haggard quest,
All in gray fur and velvet dressed. . . .

At midnight through the vaulted roof
She heard armed steps of ringing proof ;
She heard a charger's iron hoof.

The leaded lattice banked one glare
Of moonlight in the frosty air ;—
Hag shapes delayed her everywhere.

Sir Elid in the moonlight's beam,
Stiff, staring as if still a-dream,
Rode downward to the rushing stream.

In casque and corselet was he dressed,
And sang like one in goodly jest,
" I ride upon my love's last quest."

Straight onward by some mighty will
Into the river that should kill
He rode and sang, and so was still.

Not wider than its eyes are his
That stare, where icy eddies kiss
His lips, where all the horror is.

Strong through the reeds the snow seems blown.
What leans above him still as stone,
And laughs as when the night-winds moan?

If thou shouldst find him, O beware
Thy kiss ! for where the death 's most fair,
Helis, Helis, *she* kissed him there !

1885.

THE SON OF EVRAWC.

BEYOND the walls, past wood and twilight field,
  The Usk slipped onward under wharf and wall
Of old Caerlleon, rolling in, it seemed,
The heathen blood of all of Arthur's wars.
So she had left him, and he leaned alone
Within the carven casement, where a ray
Of sunset laid a bleeding spear athwart
The dark oak hall and made the arras drip.
And now life's bitterness took Peredur
By all his heart's strings, smiting. He would go,
Equipped for quest, through all the savagery
Of mountain and of forest. And this girl—
Forget her! and— her game of shuttlecock ;
This Angharad ; this child the Court had spoiled !
And he remembered how he once had rode,
Spurring his piebald stallion down the square
Upon the King's quest, and a girl had laughed
From some bedragoned balcony of walls
That faced the gateway ; and in passing he
Had glimpsed her beauty ; it was she. Befell
That snow had fallen and the winter wood
Lay carpeted with silence. And he rode
Into a vista where a raven lay
Slain of a hawk ; some blood-drops dyed the snow :
He lost himself in quaint comparisons,

Of how the sifted drift was as her skin ;
The raven's feathers as her heavy hair ;
And in her cheeks the health of maidenhood
Red as the blood-drops : so he sat and dreamed :
When one rode up in angry steel and spoke
Thrice to no answer, and in anger dashed
A gauntlet in his face and made at him :
And how he slew him and rode over him
Fiercer than fire : how he had returned
To find her fairer than their Gwenddolen,
Crowned beauty of the beautiful at Court,
With Gwenhwyvar, and fair among the fair.

And while he mused he thought he heard her voice :
Or was it fancy teasing him to hear
Her lute below the creepered walls, whose leaves
Bathed with continual sunset all the court,
Beside the ceaseless whisper of the foam
Of many fountains. Sweeter mockery
Had never held him : and he heard her sing :

" Ask me not now to sing to thee
   Songs I have loved to sing before !
I love thee not ; it can not be ;
   The dream is done ; the song is o'er.

" Yet hold my hands ; look deep into
   The heartbreak of my eyes that bore
Glad welcome erst and now adieu,
   Adieu in eyes thou dost adore.

"And thou shalt kiss my mouth and brow ;
  Smooth through my hair hands as of yore
When once 't was love and I and thou
  Forevermore, forevermore.

"Thou shalt not weep; I will not weep ;
  I love thee not ; should I regret ?—
Nay ! let me sing my songs and sleep,
  Sleep and forget, sleep and forget."

"O bird of spring," he said, "when flowers are
    gone
Thy song will winter underneath the pine :
God give thou find no winter in thy heart
Whenas dost find the frost invades thy voice !
Ah, lovelier than thy song, one sings of thee
Long ballads in each heartbeat, but in vain :
Thou dost not heed, thou wilt not hear his songs.
Or if thou dost 't is very wantonness
Whose interest apes indifference ; or words,
A moiety, of mockery ; and this
To one who 'd love thee over all belief,
Above all women and against all men."

She thrummed her lute. He listened and then
    laughed,
"Love's life ! Our Dagonet might teach me sense,
The folly that I am !—What ! have I slept
A sennight in the taking of the moon,

Or danced sleep-footed with the forest fays !
One would imagine . . . No ! . . . O silken skirts
Of wantonness ! whose devil's influence
Parades Caerlleon corridors with lies
And vanity, coquet the faithless court
Into a harlot !—Ho ! a page, a page !—
God's wounds ! my horse, my arms ; I will away ! "

And many knights he passed, nor saw ; who asked
What quest he rode. Inscrutable deeds behind
His visor, and along his sullen spear
Adventure bitter as a burning ray,
Into the night he galloped with the stars. . .

And one lone night two years thereafter.—Lost
Within a forest wilder than wild Dean,
With neither wind nor water through its leaves,
That hung as turned to stone above the moss
And grass, that wrapped the scaly rocks, death-
    dry,
And barren torrents ; where he had not found
Or man or hut, or slot of boar or deer
Through miles and miles of lamentable trees
And twisted thorns ; beneath the autumn moon,
Pale as a nun's face seen in cloistered walks,
Above dead tree-tops, like the rugged rock
Of melancholy cliffs, he saw wild walls
Of some vague castle thrust weird battlements
And hoary towers like a wizard's dream.

Great greedy weeds and burs and briers packed
Its moat and roadway ; at the very gate
Weeds deeper than a man ; their ancient stalks
Devoured with the dust and spider webs,
Or smothered with the slime where croaked the
    toad.
And Peredur against the portal rode,
And with his spear-point beat upon its bolts
A sounding minute. But no wolf-hound barked,
Only dull echoes of interior walls
And hollow rock that arched the empty halls.
And once again his truncheon shook the gate
And roused a round-eyed owl that screamed and
    blinked,
Like some fierce gargoyle, on the bartizan ;
And from a crevice, like an omen, hurled
A frantic bat. And then he heard a grate,
Concealed within the gloomy battlements,
Slid slowly, and a lean, gaunt, red-haired youth,
Lit with a link, addressed him. And he saw
That famine had sunk hollows in his cheeks,
And fixed gaunt misery in mouth and eyes.
This one retired to return again ;
Undid harsh chains and shot back stubborn
    bolts ;
And stiff with rust the snarling hinges swung.
And Peredur beheld neglected courts
Pathetic with dead leaves ; and mournful walls
Round which huge oaks thrust mistletoe and
    boughs

Of livid leaves, that seemed hooked, headlong hands
Of murder, or distorted faces come
Out of the goblin wood to scoff at him.

And he dismounted. And in clanking mail
Strode down the hall ; and in the hall beheld
Youths, lean and auburn-haired around the hearth ;
Some eighteen of an equal height, and clad
Alike in dingy garments that looked worn
And old. And these were like to him who first
Had bade him welcome. And they greeted him,
And disarrayed, and bade him to a seat.
And now an inner door flung wide ; and, lo,
Five maidens, like five forest flowers, came,
Dark-eyed, dark-haired. Behold, the queen of these
Was Angharad. Clad in a ragged robe
Of faded satin, that had once been rich.

She looked at Peredur. And he beheld
The hair again far blacker than the bird
That flies athwart the milk-white moon ; the skin
Inviolably white as wind-flowers blown
Among the mighty gospels of the trees ;
And in her cheeks, the rose of maidenhood
Red as round berries winter bushes spot
The dimpled drift with under loaded boughs.

She knew him or forgot to ask his name,
But blushed, and welcomed. And they sat and talked
Until the night waxed late. And as they talked
He marked long fasting in each face, and longed
To ask but asked not. So the night waxed late.
And then two nuns came; sandalled silence in
Frail footsteps, and pale caution on pale lips.
One brought a jar of wine, and one brought bread,
Six loaves of wheaten flour. And these said,
" God bear us witness, Lady, this is all!
Now is our Convent barren as thy board;"
And so departed. And they sat and ate. . . .

The wind upon the forest and the rain
Upon the turrets. Had he heard a sigh
Or was it but the echo of his own,
Born of great weariness, that broke his rest?
A dream, a dream. The elfin storm is on,
And sows the woods with witchcraft, and the leaves
Are chased by imps of darkness through the hail
And hurling rain; the wind is wild with leaves.
Again he slept.

        The rain among the trees,
The wind upon the turrets. Had he moaned
Now that he lay awake and heard the wind

Hoot on the towers like a green-eyed owl ?
The rain and wind ; the night is black with rain.

Upon the forest like a voice the wind ;
And on the turrets, like swift feet, the rain.
Now was he sure 't was weeping ; and arose
And found her at his door ; and took her hand,
That like a soft persuasion lay in his.
He felt long sobbings shake her and so asked :
" Tell me, my sister, wherefore dost thou weep ?"

Aud Angharad, " Yea ; I will tell thee, lord.—
My name is Angharad. My father held
An Earldom under Arthur, yea, the first
In all his Kingdom : and this palace too
Was his with cantrevs to the west and east.
When I was but a girl Earl Addanc met
And loved me. Once, when hunting, he came here
And sought my father and demanded me.
He said he loved me, and would have but me
To grace his bed and board, this Earl. But I—
I did not love him, being but a child,
My father's only child, I could not love.
And so my father said this might not be.
The Earl was wrath. I heard his furious stride
Beneath my casement ; double demons pinched
His evil eyes and twenty gnarled his face.
He cursed us ere he rode beyond our walls.
Then I was sent to Camelot and there

Became a woman of young Gwenhwyvar,
Until my father's death two years agone,
When I returned, a Countess, to find war
With Addanc here around beleagured walls.
So hath he stripped me of my appanage
Save this one keep, whose strength hath held him
      long,
Brave with my foster brothers : thou hast seen
The eighteen youths whose valor will not yield.
But what avails their valor and their will
Against hard hunger now our larder lacks,
And lacks the Convent too whereon we leaned !
And Addanc comes to-morrow morn, the truce
For our one day's deliberation done.
If he prevail—the thought is like hot hands
Here on my brain—his oath is 'that the night
Shall see me given over to his grooms.' "

She wept with tremblings.   Then said Peredur :
" Thou shalt not weep, my sister. And this Earl—
If he be early call me not too late.
Fear not.   I will not go until my sword
Hath crossed the sword of so much wickedness,
And proved this base ambition. Go and sleep." . . .

A morning gray with mist that gathered drops
Of drizzle on uncomfortable leaves.
And now the mist divided : ghostly mail,
Spears and limp pennons, and the shadowy steeds

Of shadowy knights and chieftains. And it seemed
A phantom army come to lay dim siege
To phantom walls whose warriors were ghosts.
Afar a bugle flourished in the fog,
Disconsolate, no echo of the wood
To bear its music burden. To the moat
Advanced a herald. And within the wall
The grate was opened, and the gaunt-eyed youth
Held parley with him, "How the Earl would make
End of the long dispute to-day, and leave,
Twixt three a single combat to decide."

So Peredur bade arm him, and prepare
His horse for battle ; and bade give their Earl
His answer for the Castle, " That one knight
Would try the hauberks of the banded three."

And he rode forth : and one rode up and scoffed,—
A knight in russet armor with loud words,—
" Small means to large results, forsooth ! Thou
    boast !
A vicious palate hath thy appetite,
That feasted long with hunger and must now
Conclude the banquet with three deaths !—Sir
    Death,
Here is thy death ! " and hacked at Peredur
A weighty stroke that gashed his chain camail.
But, rising in stiff stirrups, ere he passed
Two-handed swung the sword of Peredur,

And helm and head of him who fell were twain,
Split like an apple. And the walls were glad.

Then came another clad in silver mail
As he were Galahad, and in the mist
Glimmered like moonlight. And with levelled
    spear
Demanded: "Whence and what art thou? This
    stroke
Was never fathered by long fasting."—Then
Quoth Peredur, "I am of Arthur's Court."—
"A goodly service truly that of his!
Know, all his knights that I have met have died."—
Quoth Peredur: "Thy falsehood choke thee dead!
Between thy teeth, liar, I nail thy lie!"
And at his gorget hurled his ponderous spear
Ere that one met him spurring at full speed
Disdainful. And the desperate stroke of him
Who had worked wonders with the Table Round,
Glanced shattering from the sloping shield, while he,
Bent o'er his stallion's crupper, rolled; his tongue
Cleft at the root. And all the walls were glad.

Now came a third: a black knight and a black
Enormous steed. No words he wasted. But,
The fierce spears splintered, from the baldrics
    burned
Swift blades; and Battle held his breath awhile
To watch the great shields rock beneath great blows,

Oppose, deploy, as hilt to hilt they hewed
At heaume and gorget. And the battle bright
Upon the splintered greaves from many wounds.
Then Peredur, his whole strength wrenching at
Unyielding effort of his foeman's shield,
Beat down his guard and smote—And Addanc lay
Beneath the son of Evrawc whose swift hands
Razed off his casque and laid a blind blade bare
Across hot eyes, and set a heel of steel
Upon his throat and said : " Thou coward curse !
What woman wilt thou war with now ?—'T is well
Thy features are thus evil and might breed
Nightmares among the scullions, or thou
Hadst been one span the shorter !—Villainy,
Out of thy ugly head speak ! " . . . Cursing he,
A stricken bulk, growled, " Let me live " ; and so
The sword slid from fierce eyes and from his neck
The heel. And he arose to make in full
Due restitution of her lands to her
He had harassed and robbed. And so in time
This was fulfilled.

But Peredur remained,—
For, to be near her and to do for her
Was almost happiness,—until the land
Acknowledged her with all obedience.—
Her rights established, what more now remained
To lend excuse unto his long delay ?—
And so he went to her and sought her from

Among her maidens, and bespoke her how
"He would ride hence and would but say farewell."

"Dost thou then so desire?" she. And he
Ground iron strides along the lofty hall
And so returned with iron strides and said:
"Ay, by my God! Who knows I have not fought
For thee but still against thee. 'T is my curse.
I came not here to woo. Thou wouldst but laugh.—
Haply thou hast forgotten—yea, thou hast—
A son of Evrawc, Evrawc of the North,
Who loved thee once . . . hast memory of him yet? . . .
Look in his eyes once more and say farewell."

"This shall not be, my soul." He heard her low
Voice pleading softly, and new life leapt up:
He heard her as men hear the voice of hope
Upon despair's black brink, and see one star
Bloom, like a lily with a heart of fire
Throbbing within it, slowly out of night.
And each word was as welcome as a rose
Dropped from the rosy lips of laughing Spring:
"I have remembered; think'st thou I have not?—
O son of Evrawc, thou who couldst not read,
'Neath bells of folly and a merry mask,
A girl's dear secret through her tinsel acts.—

Or, was not thine but fancy?—Ah, too true,
I heard the vapid ending of a tale
Coquetry had begun for different end.—
But, if thou wilt, we can read on ; mayhap
It ends in wedlock.—Both were wrong. The one :
Because his love was blind, impetuous,
Nor saw the love that would have proved 't was
    love,
Not lust, before surrender. Th' other : that
She sought for wisdom in the frivolous,
And so made falsehood of her heart's high truth,
Deceived more than deceiving.—Wilt thou go?"

He had no rhetoric to make reply ;
Only his arms around her, and his eyes
Upon her eyes, and kisses on her mouth.
Long time they stood.—Outside the sunset flung
Barbaric glory on the autumn wood.—
And lifting up her face he said to her :—
"Thou hast thy lute? Come, let me sing to thee.
Then shalt thou sing thy song, and if it please
No better than two years agone, why, love,
We will—ride forth together to the Queen :
And Gwenhwyvar shall kiss thee and confess
Thou art her fairest flower of loveliness,
And give thee to me who will wear thee here."

TORQUEMADA.

WHAT doth the Archbishop, his chapter, of
    Toledo? Do they doze and yawn above
Some dull dry bull Pope Sextus sent to rot?
I cry, Awake! O prelates militant!
Spain's king is less than king as I am less
Than Paul! — (And what a distance!) — Look
    around ;
Observe and dare!—I write above my seal,
A grave Dominican, to postulate
Pacheco, Marquis de Villena, croaks
Wise truth into your excellencies' ears :
King Henry's heir *is* illegitimate !
Blanche of Navarre cast off, his Impotence
Gave us a wanton out of Portugal
For queen ; Joanna, who bore him this heir
The cuckold king parades, a bastard, now.
Look ! all the Court laughs—secretly ; but masks
Are but for slaves ; the people's smile is free
Of all concealment ; and the word still wags
About this son, who is his favorite's,
Bertrand la Cueva's ; whom the king himself
Made warm familiar with Joanna's bed.
Sweet infamy ! Absolve one—at the stake !

Confess the other—with the axe that hews
The neck of state asunder ! Is it well,
Prelates and ministers ?

      Be merciful !—
Lest the disease of this delicious fruit,
Our Kingdom of Castile, corrode the core,
Why not pare off all rottenness and leave
The healthy pulp ! The throne, the populace,
The Church, and God demand the overthrow,
Deponement or the abnegation of
This Henry, named the Fourth, the impotent !—
Alphonso lives. (It is my guarded hope
That brothers of such kings have no long life.)—
Am I impatient ? 't is the tonsure helps.
My native town, Valladolid, did sow
The priestly germ, ambition : there it had
Poor soil indeed, and blew to Cordova,
And sunned its torpor in a woman's smile,
And grew a tenderness too insecure
When frosts were out. Required hardiness,
And found it there at Zaragossa ; (where
Fat father Lopés, bluff Dominican,
My youth confuted with wise nonsense, and
Astonished Spain with disputation in
The public controversies of the monks.)
Transplanted to the Court, O splendid speed !
Sure hath its growth been. Now a Cardinal's
   red
Is promised by the bud that tops its stem.

My Isabella, daughter and dear child ;
The incarnation of my dear ideal ;
Pure crucifix of my religious love ;
Sweet cross which my ambition guards and holds ;
How have I through the saintly medium
Of the confessional impressed thy ear !
Ploughed up the early meadows of thy soul
For fruitful increase ! In thy maiden heart
Insinuated subtleties of seed
Shall ripen to a queen crowned with a crown
From welded gold of Arragon and Castile !
How I this son of John, the Second named,
Prince Ferdinand of swarthy Arragon,—
(Grant absolution, holy mother mine !
Thus thy advancement and thy mastery
Would I obtain !)—have on her fancy limned
In morning colors of proud chivalry !
Till he a sceptred paladin of love
And beaming manhood stands! She dreams, she dreams
What—Heaven knows ! 'T is, haply, of a star
She saw when but a babe and in the arms
Of some sad nurse. A star that laughed above
A space of Moorish balcony that hung
Above a water full of upset stars,
Reflected glimmers of old palace fêtes ;
A star she reached for, cried for, claimed and claimed
But never got ; that blew young promises,
Court promises, centupled from the tips

Of golden fingers at her infant eyes.—
Well! when this girl is grown to be a queen
What if one, Torquemada, clothe her star
In palpable approach and give it her!—

When she is queen, three steadfast purposes
Have grown their causes to divine results.
No young imagination did I train
With such endeavor and for no reward.—
How oft I told her of the gifts of kings
And queens, while pensively she sat and heard
Absorbed upon my face! her missal, crushed
'Neath one propped elbow, its bent careless leaves
Rich with illuminated capitals
Of gold and purple, open on her lap.
Felicity discoursed of who adhere
To God's true Vicar and our Holy Church:
Beatitude and all the ceaseless bliss,
Celestial, of eternal Paradise,
As everlasting as the hearts that have
Protected Heaven and its only Faith:—
" Walk not on ways that lead but to despair,
The easy ways of Satan; rather thorns
For naked feet that will not falter if
Retentive of the arm of our true Church,
Who urges weariness with comfortings
Low whispered in the tuneless ear of Care."—
" Do some digress?"—"Oh, many, many, yea!
And there's necessity! we should annul,
Pluck out the canker that contaminates,

Destroys the milk-white beauty of our rose.
God's persecution! they confront our faith
With brows of stigmatizing error writ
In Hell's red handwriting.   Shall such persist?
No! Heaven demands an end to all this shame!"—
Her pledge she gave me then: "When queen, for Spain
The Inquisition!   Let the saints record!
A mattock of deracination to
Extirpate Heresy."—And I?—Oh, I
But Torquemada a Dominican! . . .

Blind Spain hastes blindly onward, happy for
Her hellward plunge.   Our need is absolute.
Conclusion to these monster heresies
Or their most imminent consequence!   The throne,
Which is derived directly from high God,
Meseems should champion God in any cause;
And if it will not, we will teach it to.—
O Spain, Spain, Spain! awake! start up and crush
These multiplying madnesses that mouth
Their paradoxes at the Cross and shriek
Black blasphemies e'en in the face of Christ!—
O miserable Religion, is thy pride
So fallen here! thy tenement of strength
So powerless!   Then where's security,
When steadfast principle is insecure,
And God's own pillars rock and none resists?—
But I have tempered, at a certain heat,
A heart of womanhood; and have so wrought

The metal of a mind within the forge
Of holy discourse, that Toledo's steel
Springs not so true as my reforming sword,
Which carves out worship to a perfect whole.—
Imperial Isabella ! patroness !
Protectress of pure faith ! sweet Catholic !
Our Church's dear concern ! its bell ! its book !
Tribunal and its godly Act of Faith ! . . .

This need is first : to make her sceptred queen
Of wide Castile. To make, (the second need),
Him, whom Ximenes, my friend Cordelier
Shall serve as minister, King Ferdinand,
Her wedded consort. And the third great need,
The last,—which still is first,—to scour from Spain
These Moors, who make a brimstone-odious lair
Of that rich region of Granada, which
Like some vile sore of scaly leprosy
Scabs Spain's fair face.
      Delay not. Let the Church
Divide attention then 'twixt heretics
And unclean Jews. So wash her garments clean !—
King Henry falls. God and St. Dominick
Aid my endeavor ! and the Holy See
Build firm foundations !—Let the corner-stone
Of our most holy Inquisition here
Be mortared with the blood of heretics
That its strong structure may endure !—(And I ?—
Made Grand Inquisitor and Cardinal !)

AN EPISODE.

I.

SAINT DOMINICK, Pope Innocent,
   Thou holy host, Lyons once bent
 On Languedoc, may God the Father
Plunge you in everlasting Hell!
And may the blood of those who fell
   At Béziers together gather
In torrents of eternal pain,
And on your souls beat boiling rain!

II.

And Mountfort!—It was given me,
For I had prayed incessantly,
   To be the David to this giant.—
An Albigensian warrior
My husband was. He, in the war,
   The Pope had thundered on defiant
Thoulouse and outlawed Languedoc,
Stood with Earl Raymond like a rock.

III.

The walls of Béziers cried loud
And Carcassonne's, red in their cloud

Of blood, disease, and conflagration,
For vengeance !—When he left me here,
With my two babes, I felt no fear.
   The crusade's excommunication
Poured down its holy Catholics
To crush and burn us heretics.

IV.

At Carcassonne he fell. And there
My babes died famished. And despair
   And torture mine within their prison !
Till Mother of our God portrayed
This Mountfort's death. On me were laid
   Blessed hands of power in a vision.
The saints' own cause could I refuse,
That led me to besieged Thoulouse ?

V.

No arrow mine, no arbalist ;
A sling, a stone, a woman's wrist
   God and his virgin Mother aided.—
Their engines rocked our walls. I felt
The time had come and, praying, knelt ;
   Then from the sling my hair had braided
Launched at De Mountfort's bassinet
The rock where eyebrow eyebrow met.

VI.

Not mine his death. Of Carcassonne
Our Lady's hand had aimed the stone,
   That slew this monster that was master!—
Saint Dominick and Innocent,
A woman was the instrument,
   Our Holy Lady's the disaster!
Two armies saw her whirl the sling,
And afterward—no human thing.

THE MAMELUKE.

I.

SHE was a queen.   'Midst mutes and slaves,
    A mameluke, I loved her.—Waves
Dashed not more hopelessly the paves
    Of her high marble palace-stair
    Than lashed my love my heart's despair.—
As souls in Hell dream Paradise,
    I suffered, yet forgot me there
Beneath Rommaneh's houri eyes.

II.

A slave who ate his own mad heart
And served her beauty, but might dart
No amorous glance at any part.—
    I found her on a low divan,—
    Taïfi leather's perfumed tan,—
Beneath her, cushions stuffed with down;
    A slave-girl with an ostrich fan
Sat by her in a golden gown.

III.

" O boy, thy lute!"—Fair lutanist,
She loved my voice.—Beside her wrist,

Hooped with a blaze of amethyst,
   Her balass-ruby-crusted lute:
   Gold-welted stuff, like some rich fruit,
Her raiment, diamond-showered, rolled
   Folds pigeon-purple, whence one foot
Drooped in an anklet-twist of gold.

IV.

I sat and sang with all the fire
That boiled within my blood's desire,
That made me more than slave and higher:
   And at the end my passion durst
   Quench with one burning kiss its thirst.—
O eunuchs! had her face a scorn
   When through this heart your daggers burst?
And dare ye say I died forlorn?

THE SLAVE.

HE waited till within her tower
    Her taper signalled him the hour.

He was a prince both fair and brave.
What hope for him to love *her* slave!

He of the Persian dynasty;
And she the Queen of Araby!—

No Peri singing to a star
Upon the sea were lovelier.

I helped her drop the silken rope.
He clomb aflame with love and hope.

I drew the dagger from my gown
And cut the ladder, leaning down.

Oh, wild the face, and wild the fall;
Her cry was wilder than them all.

I heard her cry, I heard him groan,
And stood as merciless as stone.

The eunuchs came ; fierce scimitars
Stirred in the torch-lit corridors.

She spoke like one who prays in sleep,
And bade me strike or she would leap.

I bade her leap, the time was short ;
And kept the dagger for my heart.

She leapt. I put their blades aside
And smiling in their faces—died.

THE SEVEN DEVILS OF MAHOMET.

THERE is a legend, lost in some old dusty
    Tome of the East, — and who shall question it ?—
Concluding ancient wisdom, rather musty,
    Wherein much war and wickedness and wit
    Insult and wrath and love and shame are writ.
Wherein is written that, when Mahomet
    Fled out of Mecca from the people's wrath,
    He met a shadow standing in his path,
A naked horror blacker than hewn jet.

It in one hand held out a flaming jewel,
    Wherein fierce colors burnt and blent like eyes
Of seven fires as a single fuel:
    The horror said, "God cursed them for their lies.
    These are the seven devils of the wise
And I am Satan!" And the Prophet saw
    The purposes of Allah, and replied,
    "God, set them free! And what shall be denied
To these except life's hope?" His word was law.

Since then the seven devils have descended
    From nation unto nation past the ken

Of Mahomet, who left us undefended
   Of any amulet of sword or pen
   'Gainst demons boring at the brains of men :
So many maggots that will spend their spite
   In sadness, fear and scorn, despair and rage,
   Envy and jealousy, on fool and sage,
The seven devils with us day and night.

JOHN DAVIS, BOUCANIER.

HIGH time, high time, good gentlemen, to sail
    the Spanish Main !
Three months we've watched for galleons and treas-
    ure bound for Spain ;
Three months ! and not a vessel, neither barque nor
    brigantine !
No Cartagena plate-ship or De Dios have we
    seen !
Our sails sleep idle as the wind, our ships as gulls
    or waves ;
And shall inaction rot us like a gang of shackled
    slaves !
Up, Boucaniers ! the land is wide and wider far the
    sea—
Somewhere between the dusk and dawn and dusk
    some hope must be ;
Some ship somewhere or city there beneath the
    Indian sky,
What matter whether east or west or if men live or
    die,
Or fight or yield on ship or field !—The main for
    me and mine !—
To cram our ports against their ports and see the
    battle-line

Pour on their decks with naked necks the dirks between our teeth;
And sail or sink our flag is there, we Boucaniers beneath!

And what availed your patron saints, Iago or Saint Marc,
Lanceros, Adelantados, against Ravenau's barque!
O butchers of good Jean Ribault, well might your cheeks turn pale
When Montebaro's brigantine shook to the breeze her sail!
Around the coasts where New Spain boasts the haughtiness of Old,
Her tyranny and bigotry and sordid greed for gold,
From east to west and north to south among the Carib Isles,
Swift as revenge the Frenchman swept across the foaming miles.
The spirit of Pierre-le-Grand and of his gallant crew,
Who took a galleon with a boat, be with me and with you!

Prime arquebus and sharpen blade, and let the guns look brave
As burnish of the sunlight's beam upon the sun-lit wave!

And all be glad as when we had Granada in our
    hold,
And stabbed the city's sentinels and took the city's
    gold :
New Spain's good homes and churches, aye, will
    not forget too soon
The Boucanier, John Davis, he who taught their
    Dons a tune,
Dutch serenades to frighten maids beneath the
    yellow moon.
What helped the Latin of their monks to curse
    what Satan blessed !
Bright pieces, broad, -of-eight and plate we counted
    in our chest.
And now that we may double or may treble every
    piece,
Pipe up the anchor, boatswain ! and before the
    hawser cease,
Let every sail salute the gale and every rope be
    taunt,
The Devil take all care and—us, if jaundiced colors
    daunt !

The sea-gulls dip and dive and float, and swim and
    soar again,
Be merry, merry gentlemen, and drink " the Ships
    of Spain ! "
High-hearted as the sea-gulls soar, and as the case
    may go,

A round Dutch oath for wealth and health and—to
  Spain's overthrow.
Doff caps and follow ; though the prize be overfat
  or lean,
Kneel down and give her thanks who leads, Dame
  Fortune who is queen !
Upon our prow she guides us now against San
  Augustine.

THAMUS.

AND it is said that Thamus sailed
   Off islands of Ægean seas
No seamen yet had ever hailed,
   No merchant yet had sailed to these,
   Phœnician or the Chersonese.

And lying all becalmed, 't is told,
   How wonderful with peace that night
Rolled out of dusk and dreamy gold
   One star, whose splendor seemed to write
   Laws that were mightier than might.

Like shadows on a shadow-ship
   The dark-haired, dark-eyed sailors lay,
When from the island seemed to slip,
   Borne overhead and far away,
   A voice that " Thamus ! " seemed to say.

Then silence ; and the languid Greek,
   The lounging Cretan, watched the sky,
Or in carousal ceased to speak
   And sing. Again came rolling by
   The voice, and " Thamus ! " in its cry.

All were awake : tall, swarthy men
   With bated breath stood listening,
Or gravely scanned the shore. And then,
   Although they saw no living thing,
   Again they heard the summons ring.

And " Thamus ! " sounded shore and sea ;
   And at the third call leaned the Greek
Full facing toward the isle; and he
   Cried to the voice and bade it speak
   The mission, message it would seek.

" Thou shalt sail on to such a place
   Among the pagan seas," it said,
" To such a land ; and thou shalt face
   Against it when the east is red,
   And cry aloud ' Great Pan is dead ! ' " . . .

As fearful of unholy word
   Their souls stood stricken with strange fear. . . .
Then Thamus said, "Yea, I have heard.
   Yet 't is my purpose still to steer
   Straight on. That land shall never hear !"

And so they sailed that night ; and came
   Into an unknown sea ; and there
The east burnt like a sword of flame
   A Cyclops forges ; straight the air
   Lay sick with calm ; the morn was fair.

Then double dread was theirs ; and dread
 Was Thamus' ; and he raised his hand
And shouted, "Pan ! great Pan is dead !"
 And all the twilight-haunted land
 Cried, "Pan is dead !" from peak to strand.

They saw pale shrines and temples nod
 Among the shaken trees ; and pale
Wild forms of goddess and of god
 Crawl forth with crumbling limbs and trail
 Woe, till the dim land grew one wail.—

What tripods groaned ?—Serapis first
 Within Canopus' temples heard
The word, and his brute granite burst
 A monster bulk. Dodona stirred
 And bowed huge oaks before the word,

That left them thunder-riven. Fell
 On Aphaca where, marble-hewn,
The marble Venus had a well
 That burnt white fire like a moon—
 And, lo ! her loveliness lay strewn.

Then o'er Cilicia passed, and bent
 Sarpedon's oracle with scorn,
Apollo—Yea ! the god lay rent,
 And Delphos dumb. And, lo ! the morn
 O'er Bethlehem where Christ lay born.

ADVENTURERS.

SEEMINGLY over the hill-tops,
    Possibly under the hills,
A tireless wing that never drops,
    And a song that never stills.

Epics heard on the star's lips?
    Lyrics read in the dew?—
To be the song at our finger tips,
    And live the world anew!

Cavaliers of the Cortés kind,
    Bold and stern and strong,—
And, oh, for a fine and muscular mind
    To sing a new world's song!

Sailing seas of the silver morn,
    Winds of the balm and spice,
To put the old-world art to scorn
    At the price of any price!

Danger, death, but the hope high!
    God's, if the purpose fail!
Into the deeds of a vaster sky
    Sailing a dauntless sail.

VOYAGERS.

WHO will tell me where the pale
    Blossoms of our childhood blow ?—
Levels under hills that trail
    Morning summits in the glow,
Crimson, o'er a crimson sail ?

Whence our manhood entered on
    The unknowable, unseen ;
Cavaliers who still have gone
    Sailing a frail brigantine
On from voyaging dawn to dawn.

Leons seeking lands of song,
    Fabled fountains spouting spray
Where their anchors drop among
    Corals of some blooming bay,
And the swarthy natives throng.

" Shoulder axe and arquebuse ! "—
    Rolls the region past yon range
Of sierras, vaporous,
    Rich with gold and wild and strange,
Still evading them and us.

Who may find it ?—Though your zeal
   Darien summits doth subdue,
Your Balboa eyes reveal
   But a vaster sea come to ;
New endeavor for your keel.

Yet !—who sails with face set hard
   Westward, while reward still flies
Eastward, where the starbeams sward
   Meadows of the graveless skies,
He may find it—afterward.

AMERICA.

THESE are the days when Strength sits wisdom-
    lipped,
  With eagle thoughts that soar above the storm
    Convulsing ledges of the rocks of Wrong.
O Liberty, thy tongue is thunder-tipped ;
  Thy words are senates that can slay or charm ;
    Thy voice is battle in a freedom song.

America, what hates may touch thy hands !
  Disdains insult thy majesty of brow !
    Oppressions brave the mercy of thine eyes !—
Behind thee dies the darkness from the lands !
  Before thee mounts the glory of the Now !
    Around thee sit the sessions of the skies !

These are the days when Progress leans to heed
  The lessons of the heavens and of God,
    The golden texts of morning and of night :
The science of the suns hath taught her speed !
  No precedent of kingdoms makes her nod !
    Brow-bound with bolts, her feet are shod with
      light !

America, beneath thy awful heel
  What iron tyrannies, that crushed the poor,
    Writhe scorpion lengths abolished with their ire !—
Around thine arms, that are not wrapped in steel,
  What old-world injuries have failed to moor
    Barques thou hast beacon'd like a pillar'd fire !

Dark Monarchies, the darker days divide,
  And swords of Superstition and of Lust
    Fall shattered from the necks of Truth and Mind.—
One onward principle, achieving pride ;
  One starward purpose over empires' dust
    Strewn with the fetters that no more shall bind.

Humanity, thy human gyves are rent ;
  The Christian actual looks up again
    Through God-progressions of eternity :
Behold ! the pagan, Violence, is spent !
  His idol, Ignorance, lies burst in twain
    Before the splendor of the Christ to be !

THE OCKLAWAHA.

RIVER, winding from the west,
   Winding to the River May,
Often hath the Indian pressed
Through your black-gums and your mosses,
Where the alligator crosses
   Still some lily-paven bay,
Basking there in lazy rest.

Still the spider-lily loops
   Sprawling flowers, peels of pearl,
Where the green magnolia stoops
Buds to yellow-lily bonnets;
Where, the morning dew upon its
   Golden funnels, curl on curl
The festooning jasmine droops.

Who may paint the beauty of
   Orchids blooming late in June,
Bristling on the boughs above!
Cypress-trees where many a flower
Long lianas' tendrils shower
   On the deer that come at noon
Muzzles in cool depths to shove.

Lilied inlets where the teal
   Dabble 'mid the water-grasses,
That some treasure seem to seal
With white blooms that star the river:
Bays the swift kingfishers shiver
   Into circles as each passes
O'er their mirrors that reveal.

Bends, reflecting root and moss,
   Where the tall palmettoes throng,
Over live-oaks tower and toss
Panther necks whose heads are heavy:
Hamaks where the perfumes levy
   Tribute from the birds in song,
From the mocking-birds that cross.

Logs the turtles haunt; and deeps
   Of lagoons the searching crane
Wades; and where the heron sleeps;
Where the screaming limpkins listen,
And the leaping mullet glisten;
   Bream and bass dart by again,
And the dark didapper sweeps.

Coäcoochee, Coäcoochee,
   Still the huge magnolias bloom
And the tangled Cherokee,
Where the blazing-star spreads splendor

Through the forest, and the tender
   Discs of the hibiscus loom,
Trailing over bush and tree.

Osceola, Osceola,
   Phantoms of your vanquished race
From the starlight seem to draw
Stern invasion. Mossy regions
Swarm the Seminole's lost legions,
   Threatening war-paint on each face.—
Dead, long dead for Florida !

THE MINORCAN.

I.

THE mocking-bird may sing
    Loud welcomes in the spring ;
The farewell of our nightingales
    Prevails, prevails !
No grief may hush their song :
In sleep they sing the clearer—
It 's " home, home, home," the whole night
    long—
What wonder that we feel our wrong
    The nearer !

II.

Hibiscus blooms surprise
The swamp with rosy eyes ;
The Balearic girl but knows
    Our rose, our rose !
No slavery may undo
Her dream it makes the purer,
With " love, love, love," the long night
    through,—
To make the day's long heartbreak too
    The surer.

III.

The wind from out the west
Would teach our souls unrest ;
We will not hear until hath ceased
    The East, the East !
No sorrow wakes to weep
But th' olive's whisper hushes ;
It 's " rest, rest, rest," while night doth
    keep
The weight of memory asleep
    That crushes.

IV.

Deep ocean brings us shells ;—
Adieus and dead farewells,
Surf-couriers of its swiftest foam
    From home, from home !
But when the stars are high,
Its slumberous voices cherish
The heart with " hope," that will deny
Despair until we wake to sigh
    Or perish.

THE SPRING IN FLORIDA.

CRAB-APPLES make the western belt
  Of hamak one gay holiday of pink,
And through palmetto depths, on breaths like felt,
  The jasmine odors sink.

There blows a blur of peach and pearl
  Around the villa by the river's side;
The guava blossoms and the orange-trees whirl
  Aroma far and wide.

    " He courts her!" sings the mocking-bird,
    " He courts her, and she misses
    This word or that she might have heard,
    Had he not drawn a sweeter word
      From her sweet lips with kisses.
        He courts her!"

Chameleons bask bright bodies there,
  Where lemons powder stars above the way;
The fragrance holds its heart out and the air
  Embalms it in a ray.

Strange lilies laugh mute mouths of musk
  And stun the zephyr, where the loaded light

Shines with japonicas. And tusk on tusk
   Magnolias bud in sight.

     The red-bird's song is, "Haste, haste, haste!
       Nor wait till morn to marry—
     Mayhap you 'll find hath gone to waste
     The poppy that the stalk once graced:
       The moments may not tarry,
          So marry!"

There the verandah, spilled and spun
   With deep bignonia, bulging one full frame
Of scarlet foam, seems pouring for the sun
   A cataract of flame.

The oleander hedges soak
   The dusk with sweetness; and the gray moss
       heaps
Ghost raiment round the aloe and live-oak
   Where the bronze fountain leaps.

     "Oh, love, love, love!" the wood-dove coos,
      "Oh, love, love, love forever!
     They, who the crimson rose refuse,
     The lily's whiteness too may lose—
       So choose thou now or never!
       Oh, love, love, love!"

STRATEGY.

AND is it madness still to hope
    For ways made blue with vetchlings' eyes,
Beyond the creek-road and the slope
    Far as the gray hawk flies?

A bird may beat a crippled wing
To lure me from its brush-built nest;
A sudden throat may sit and sing
    Its wildwood happiest.

Beyond the orchard hills be hills
Of knee-deep huckleberries, green
With little bell-blooms, summer fills
    To plumpness of the bean.

O season of the sassafras!
O animal, the rathe months hold,
Kick happy heels in deeps of grass
    And roll in deeper gold!

Confusing strategy! for frost
With ice seams every flower-bed!
Where once each stalk an Edgar tossed,
    Tom shakes a shivering head.

Where once the gladiola shook
A wand of folly in the sun,
That humped stock hath a grizzly look—
    The poor, pale Fool is done.

A sorry beard my rose-bush hath,
An old king's, where the sleet 's a tear
For this dead lily in my path—
    Cordelia and Lear.

THE WHIPPOORWILL.

I.

ABOVE long woodland ways that led
    To dells the stealthy twilights tread
The west was hot geranium-red;
    And still, and still,
Along old lanes, the locusts sow
With clustered pearls the Maytimes know,
Out of the crimson afterglow,
We heard the homeward cattle low,
And then the far-off, far-off woe
    Of " whippoorwill ! " of " whippoorwill ! "

II.

Beneath the idle beechen boughs
We heard the cow-bells of the cows
Come slowly jangling towards the house;
    And still, and still,
Beyond the light that would not die
Out of the scarlet-haunted sky,
Beyond the evening-star's white eye
Of glittering chalcedony,
Drained out of dusk the plaintive cry
    Of " whippoorwill ! " of " whippoorwill ! "

III.

What is there in the moon, that swims
A naked bosom o'er the limbs,
That all the wood with magic dims?
    While still, while still,
Among the trees whose shadows grope
'Mid ferns and flow'rs the dew-drops ope,—
Lost in faint deeps of heliotrope
Above the clover-sweetened slope,—
Retreats, despairing past all hope,
    The whippoorwill, the whippoorwill.

SATAN.

STILL shall I stand the everlasting hate
   Colossal Chaos builded 'neath thine eyes,
  The symbol of all evil, that defies
Thy victory, and vanquished still can wait.
Scar me again with such vast force as late
   Hurled abrupt thunder and archangel cries
   'Mid fiery whirlwinds of the terrible skies
Down the deep's roar against Hell's monster gate!
Thy wrath cannot abolish or make less
   Me, an eternal wile opposed to wrath:
   No purpose shalt thou have and I no plan!
Behold thy Eden's vanished loveliness!
   Why hast thou set a sword within its path,
   And cursed and exiled thine own image, Man?

SIC VOS NON VOBIS.

IF on the thorns thy feet be bruised to-morrow,
   And far the fierce sands glare,
Unbind thy temples! thank life for its sorrow,
   Its longing and despair!

With love within, what heart shall fail and wither,
   Athirst for rivered hills?
Moaning, "Mine! mine! what hate hath led me
     hither
   Unto a sky that kills!"

Unworthy thou! if faith should sink and falter;
   Blind hand and blinder eye
Bind the blind hope upon thy doubt's old altar
   And stab it till it die.

Think not hast hugged no happiness and never
   Communed with lovely sleep;
Had night before thine eyeballs—night forever
   To lead thee to the deep.

Ay! wouldst thou have thy self-love for a burden,
   A fardle bound with tears,

To sweat beneath and gain at last as guerdon
   From hands of wasted years !

Coaxing lewd stars to light thee, feebler, thinner
   Than phantoms in the moon ;
Dead stars and all the darkness of the inner
   Self's deader plenilune :

To see at last,—beneath Death's sterner learning,
   —Through sockets sealed with frost,
The awful sunsets of red heavens burning
   God's baffling pentecost.

ONCE.

ONCE when the morning on the curling breakers,
    Along the foaming sand,
Flashed expectation, by the ocean's acres
    Love took command.

And so we sailed, Æolian music melting
    Around our silken sails ;
The bubbled foam our prow of sandal pelting
    With rainbow gales.

We watched the beach, with sprawling cactus hateful
    And gnarled palmetto, pass
Beyond our vision where Life once walked fateful
    With Time's slow glass.

And yet, and yet, who might forget the beauty
    Of dim and fragile shells,
That strewed sad shores of Patience and of Duty
    Like asphodels !

Harsh rocks of Care where Faith's meek flow'r suffices
    To lead Love up and on,

To levels, that the Bible's lily spices,
    Divine with dawn!

Still, still we went, Love laughing at to-morrow,
    Past sunny isle and cape;
Three were we now:—my Soul and Love and—
    Sorrow,
    A tall, grave shape.

And still we went, Love at the golden rudder,
    Till all the day lay late,
When, lo! beside him, like an icy shudder,
    Stood pallid Hate.

And still we went, Love seeing me no other:
    None crowned with bleeding thorn,
None armed with violence, and now another—
    Unyielding Scorn.

Beholding then, Love, who had once commanded
    Alone, now summoned Pride;
The darker three, against the bright two banded,
    Stood side by side.

On through the night our boat went drifting, drifting;
    My stricken soul alone,
A white face cold as moonlit marble lifting
    To moan and moan.

RESIGNATION.

IF Grief must fill my heart with tears, and Time
    Abate no hour
Of tyranny with any laughing rhyme,—
    Be Grief my dower.

If days must sing to my attentive soul
    Joy's cradle-song,
Nor lift one grave note in the lovely whole,
    O Joy, be long.

Bring me pale flowers of the handselled hills,
    To braid and lay
On coffined brows, sad separation fills
    With death's dismay.

Dreams, dreams to drug my soul's life-cup with pure
    Ideal love ;
Glad lips and eyes whose beauties still allure
    The world above.

A harp to hold between lax knees and smite
    With prayers and tears
For night bereaved by day, and day by night,
    Through bitter years.

A lute to hug unto the heart, and make
    Youth's tripping tune
Of Maytime's lily that but fades to wake
    The rose of June.

Up bars of stars, the golden notes of skies,
    On night's black page
Let the moon's music of pale pathos rise
    To teach young age.

Upon the mountains of the morning lands,
    An unsealed book
Let Love's nude childhood lift in happy hands
    And old age look.

Apportion, O my God, the hope or fear,
    The grief or glee !
Thine be the purpose of each smile, each tear
    Eternally.

AFTER RAIN.

To see the blossom-bosomed Day again,
    With all the star-white Hours in her train,
Laugh out of pearl-lights in the golden ray,
That, leaning on the woodland wildness, blends
A sprinkled amber with the showers that lay
Their oblong emeralds on the leafy ends!
To see her bend with maiden-braided brows
Above the wildflower sidewise with its strain
Of dewy happiness, to kiss again
Each drop to death! Or, under rainy boughs,
With fingers fragrant as the woodland rain,
Gather the sparkles from the sycamore,
      To set within each core
Of crimson roses girdling her hips
      Where each bud dreams and drips!

Smoothing her blue-black hair,—where many a tusk
Of iris flashes fairy falchions, sheen
Around blue banners of the Fairy Queen,—
Is it a Naiad singing in the dusk,
That haunts the spring, where all the moss is musk
With footsteps of the flowers on the banks?
Or but a wild-bird voluble with thanks?

Balm for each blade of grass : the hours prepare
A festival each weed 's invited to :
Each bee is drunken with the honied air :
And all the heaven is eloquent with blue :
The wet hay glitters, and the harvester
Tinkles his scythe,—as twinkling as the dew—
   That shall not spare
Blossom or brier in its sweeping path ;
   And, ere it cut one swath,
Rings them they die and tells them to prepare.

What is the spice that haunts each glen and glade?
A Dryad's lips, who slumbers in the shade?
A Faun, who lets the heavy ivy-wreath
Slip to his thigh as, reaching up, he pulls
The chestnut-blossoms in whole bosomfuls?
A sylvan Spirit, whose sweet mouth will breathe
Her viewless presence near us, while we wade
The brook, whose wisdom knows no other song
Than that the bird sings where it builds beneath
The wild-rose and sits singing all day long?

Oh, let me sit with silence for a space !
A little while forgetting that fierce part
Of man that struggles in the toiling mart :
Where God can look into my heart's own heart
From unsoiled heights made amiable with grace :
And where the sermons that the old oaks keep

Can steal into me.—And what better then
Than turning to the moss a quiet face
To fall asleep? a little while to sleep
And dream of wiser worlds and wiser men.

1886.

PEACE.

I.

WHEN rose-leaves 'neath the rose-bush lie,
    And lilies bloom and lilacs die,
When days fall sadder than a sigh,
      Lay me asleep
Where breezes blow the rose-leaves by,
      Lay me asleep.

II.

When to the dusty, dreary day
The lonely clouds bring cooling gray,
And languidly the tree-tops sway
      And flowers there,
The silence and the shade will pray,
      And flowers there.

III.

And shouldst thou stop, O shed no tear
To flaw the pallid peace that 's here!
The woodland whisper far and near
      That 's weary grown;
Nor bring the world to jar the ear
      That 's weary grown.

www.ingramcontent.com/pod-product-compliance
Lightning Source LLC
Chambersburg PA
CBHW020857230426
43666CB00008B/1217